HOW WOULD YOU COPE WITH THIS?

INCLUSION BODY MYOSITIS

DEMENTIA

WAYNE RAMSAY

Copyright © 2023 by Wayne Ramsay

ISBN: 978-1-77883-049-5 (Paperback)

978-1-77883-050-1 (E-book)

All rights reserved. No part of this publication may be reproduced, distributed, or transmitted in any form or by any means, including photocopying, recording, or other electronic or mechanical methods, without the prior written permission of the publisher, except in the case brief quotations embodied in critical reviews and other noncommercial uses permitted by copyright law.

The views expressed in this book are solely those of the author and do not necessarily reflect the views of the publisher, and the publisher hereby disclaims any responsibility for them.

BookSide Press
877-741-8091
www.booksidepress.com
orders@booksidepress.com

INTRODUCTION

HELLO AND WELCOME

I would like to introduce myself. My name is Wayne Ramsay. I was born in Melbourne, Australia in 1946. It is October 2022; we just got over winter and are now enjoying spring, hoping for a very nice summer. I thought it would be a good idea to share with you what happens to your body when you contract inclusion body myositis (IBM). The interesting part about writing this book is that I cannot type very well as my hands are very stiff. I cannot bend my fingers due to IBM. I'm able to type with one finger and a thumb, so it takes a while to do anything. I found a programme on my computer called "dictate." It comes free with the Windows 365 package and it allows me to turn voice into text; my voice is very husky, and the computer sometimes finds it hard to understand. I am sure it thinks I am Chinese. I am forever going back, correcting mistakes that the computer makes. Also, I am not computer-savvy; one must be very careful as to what keys are pressed so that

I don't delete any dialogue. One annoying part about this programme is when somebody else walks into the room and talks, the computer picks up everything that person has said and adds it to the text. What a bloody nuisance.

I must then go back and delete the whole lot. Someone was watching Spiderman the other day and I ended up with Spiderman dialogue in the text so really, the only place to write this book is somewhere peaceful and quiet. This is my second book. The first one was named *Roscoe, the Gold-plated Dog*, the story of my golden retriever.

I joined the Royal Australian Navy in 1963. I was only in for four years because I was a sleepwalker. Unfortunately, the two do not mix, and I was discharged in 1967. I was a cook on the destroyer HMAS Duchess during my short stint in the Navy. I was also stationed at HMAS Cerberus, the major land-based training facility in Australia. It is situated at Crib Point in Victoria, about 70 kilometres out of Melbourne. While in the Navy, I met a lovely girl by the name of Jeanette. I married her in 1968. While writing this book, we have celebrated our 54th wedding anniversary. We have two children and four grandchildren. My daughter, Jackie, who is 52, had two girls named Kayla and Bree Anna. My son, Shane, who is 50, had two boys, Clayton and Curtis. We had a big fallout with our daughter in 2021, and we no longer talk to Jackie who also turned the girls against us. They don't want anything to do with us. I look at it this way. It is her loss if she thinks I'm going to crawl up to her; she has got another thing coming. In simple terms, she has stated that she had a shit childhood and missed out on a lot. My son, on the other hand, said his childhood was great and did not miss out on anything. One is right, one is wrong?

Nothing is too much trouble for my son; he is always there for us (thank God) as we needed somebody to help us get through the last few years which have certainly tested us out with the way we are now. Anyway, we will get back to this subject later. Sit back and enjoy.

CHAPTER ONE

My journey with myositis started around 2018. That is when I first noticed a change in my left hand. I was finding it very hard to make a fist. The fingers just would not bend, I thought it could have been arthritis. My doctor, whose name is Peter, had no real idea; he had never come across symptoms like that before. He said he would investigate it. After many tests and numerous doctor's appointments, the official diagnosis came in January 2019—IBM. Inclusion body myositis. Never heard of it? Very few people have. It is one of those diseases that slips through the cracks. With all due respect, I have never come across anybody except a neurologist who knows what IBM is. Some doctors have heard of IBM but are unaware of what it does to the body. I found that most nurses are also in the same boat—never heard of it.

The next paragraph has been taken from the myositis association of Australia newsletter explaining what IBM is. Inclusion body myositis is a condition that causes muscles to become thin and weak. Symptoms usually start in middle to late life and is the most common muscle disease diagnosed after the age of 50. Nevertheless, it is still considered rare, with only between three to four people out of every 100,000 people over 50 years old having this condition.

People are starting to be aware of motor neuron disease (MND) in Australia. IBM is a cousin to MND, mainly recognized because of Neal Danaher, the ex-AFL Melbourne football club coach. He came down with the disease seven years ago. He's very lucky as most people who get MND don't last more than three years; he certainly has got a slow version. He has come across as a brave gutsy person who seems to have accepted the cards he has been dealt; he just goes along and accepts everything that comes his way. I certainly admire the way he goes about it and the way he presents himself.

People have started to take notice and not just football fans because of the big freeze slide every year on the Queen's Birthday holiday at the Melbourne Cricket Ground. Let me explain what happens: this event is held on one of the largest sporting days on the AFL calendar. It is the annual game between Melbourne Football Club and the Collingwood Football Club. What they do is install a slide, probably 2 metres wide by 8 metres long. At the bottom is a pit filled with crushed ice. The whole idea is that several celebrities are chosen to slide down and hopefully raise funds for the cause; each celebrity dresses up as anyone they like. This event takes place before the main game starts. The people who organise this event also sell woollen beanies at $25 each; last year they sold over 50,000. This event alone has raised awareness on MND. I would imagine every person at the ground, usually around 80,000 people, would know what MND was. Prior to this, no one knew nothing.

Since the big freeze has started, they have raised close to $30 million to help fight this horrid disease and even with all that money pumped into the project, it does not mean success. Unfortunately, no news of anything let alone a cure has arisen at this stage. I only hope they can find a cure for this one as it would relate very easily to IBM.

IBM is an unknown cousin of MND. It is supposed to work a lot slower and only affects the muscles in the hand's arms and legs. Unfortunately, MND affects more parts of the body including the lungs and the voice box. My cousin, Murray Swinton, was diagnosed with MND in January 2021. Unfortunately, he passed away in October 2021 at the age of 58. Talk about fast. I suppose I can be grateful that I do not have MND.

Let's look at my life prior to 2018 before IBM and go through some of the sicknesses and illnesses that I've encountered in my travels, prior to myositis. Let me explain what my personal physical shape is. I am 76 years of age, five feet and 10 inches tall (178 cm), and weigh around

80 kilos. I have a very light frame and I have a moustache, otherwise clean-cut. I drink beer socially and enjoy a stubby or two of beer at night with dinner. I smoked cigarettes for 40 odd years and gave up in 2010.

My main occupation has been a salesman selling cigarettes to the tobacconists and what they called in those days fancy goods to gift shops and anyone that sold our merchandise. I have worked for many wholesalers, selling anything from cigarette lighters, batteries, fancy goods, lolly brands such as Wizz Fizz and sherbet cones. My largest problem as a salesperson was, I called a spade a spade and told people the way it was. Often it did not go over too well with the boss. I found myself out of a job on a couple of occasions because of my big mouth.

This eventually led to me working for myself, and the last job I had was a wholesaler, selling batteries to licenced post offices. I did this for over 10 years before selling the business and retiring.

Let's go back 25 years to 1993. My first angina attack came at the ripe old age of 47 in October 1993 while grouting a tile floor. I can remember how long ago it was because we were going to renew our vows and remarry on our 25th wedding anniversary which was only three days away from the day the attack occurred. Whilst tiling on this evening, I experienced some mild chest pain but being a normal male, I naturally ignored it and continued tiling. I would then have a break, light up a smoke, and have a beer; the pain would subside then back to it. I seemed to accept the pain at the same time not knowing or realizing that this could be heart-related. It did not seem to bother my typical macho male attitude. I'll be right mate, only a little hiccup. After a couple of attacks, I gave it away and went to bed. I didn't tell Jeanette at the time, as I did not want to worry her. Also, she was not in the room at the time of the attacks and could not see my face or my reaction. Had she been in the room she would have called an ambulance for sure. All I wanted to do was finish the grouting.

Next morning, I went to clean up some of the grout and immediately had an attack which was twice as strong as I had the night before. This one really floored me. It stopped me in my tracks. I went totally white, collapsed into a chair which in turn caused us to call in the local GP. Even if we had called an ambulance we ended up with the same result. Jeanette and I were sent to Frankston Hospital emergency department. They did all the appropriate tests relating to the heart and confirmed that I had an angina attack. Frankston hospital did not have the facilities or the equipment to do angioplasties. They had to send any patient to another major hospital. They kept me in the hospital for around two weeks, while waiting for an opening at the Royal Melbourne Hospital. Imagine being in the ward, feeling pretty good as it felt there was nothing wrong with me. The treatment they gave me for my condition to keep any attacks at bay was tablets plus a daily Transiter-Nitro slow-release patch which when applied to the body releases a limited amount of glyceryl trinitrate, which causes the body to open the arteries and allow blood to travel through freely to the heart. I was told the wait could be as long as six weeks; the amount of people in hospitals around Melbourne waiting for this procedure is in the dozens. I will just have to wait for my turn. My turn finally came after a wait of just 13 days. What a waste of resources. Why couldn't they have sent me home and as soon as a vacancy came up, call me in, and send me into the royal Melbourne instead of staying in hospital, twiddling my bloody thumbs? It was a pain in the arse, sitting around waiting for an opening at Royal Melbourne where they would perform the angiogram.

    I would like the reader to imagine himself or herself. Plant in your mind that you are squatting down or actually on your knees ready to grout the floor. You have a grouting tool in your hand, you put some grout on the floor, and then you use the tool to move backwards and forwards, making sure the grout goes into the gaps between the tiles. All of a sudden, you get pain in the chest. The pain is like having a clamp opening and closing on your chest. The pain takes the wind out of your sails and stops you in your tracks. You find it very hard to breathe as the clamp continues to take your breath away. You struggle to get up, but you do and you go and sit down to try and catch your breath, hoping the pain will subside. I hope that this has given you an idea of what it was like to have an angina attack or a heart attack.

I was driven to the Royal Melbourne Hospital by a private nurse as she was on leave and heading that way anyway. She went in with me and made sure that I went to the right department. At that time, I had a loose tooth. The nurse said that if the tooth remained loose, they could not attempt to do any heart operation as it could cause a major infection. After that news, I kept moving my tooth with my finger and eventually it came out. The doctors were none the wiser so the angioplasty went ahead. The operation took an hour. The doctors inserted two stents in my arteries which were up to 80% blocked; they were the first of many to come. A private ambulance transferred me back to Frankston Hospital where I stayed for two more days, then at last, I was given the all clear and finally went home—certainly an experience which you don't want to repeat. Since my experience at Frankston Hospital, they now have the facility to treat patients that need to have angiograms and angioplasty. They do not do any of the bypass surgeries. They are only done at the very large major hospitals. Very handy saves going into the larger hospitals like the Royal Melbourne and waiting around for two weeks, wasting valuable hospital funds which could be used for something more important.

I have spoken about it but never explained what happens when you have an angiogram. This procedure is done under local anaesthetic. In my case they went into the body through the inside of the thigh. This is where your main artery is situated. If you cut there, you will bleed out within minutes. Naturally the main artery leads to the heart. The doctors place a surgical wire [catheter] into the groin, which is hollow and has little hooks. The hooks enable the doctor to grab hold of a stent if needed to be inserted and also are capable of clearing any build-up of foreign matter which may be blocking the artery by pushing it to one side which will enable the blood to continue through. The doctors guide the wire through the arteries up to the part which is blocked. Prior to the wire being placed in the body, a dye is injected into the artery so that any blockages can be seen. All this is relayed onto a TV screen in the form of X-rays so the doctors can see your heart in action.

Angioplasty is the procedure used to unblock an artery. It is called balloon angioplasty and if necessary, stenting is where a metal sleeve is used to open the blockage and is left in your artery to keep it open.

Once the procedure is finished, a nurse will have to seal the wound. The doctor or nurse has to apply pressure to the wound for at least twenty minutes. You, the patient, must remain as still as possible for between two and six hours. If the wound opens up at all, you could bleed out. If you ever wanted to commit suicide all you have to do is slice yourself on the inner thigh and get that artery. They say you can bleed out within two minutes. I don't know if it's true, and I'm not going to try it.

In December 1999, 10 days prior to Christmas, we invited some friends around as you do to join us in some drinks. We set up a spot in the backyard. I went down the side of the house to get myself an ashtray so the cigarette butts were not scattered around the yard. We had a combustion heater which burned wood. This is the spot where I chopped the wood. I had covered many of the logs with a tarpaulin so that no one could see the mess. Dickhead me forgot about the covered logs and steps on one, thus twisting my leg. *SNAP* I broke my tibia and fibular on my right leg. I should have been more careful as there was wood everywhere. My leg twisted and it broke. I landed flat on my back, tried to get up, and I felt the bone move in my leg as I tried to lift it. I called out to Jeanette and the visitors at the time, and they all came down to where I was and assisted me with a pillow and blanket to make me comfortable. They called the ambulance. For the period of when they called the ambulance and by the time they arrived, I cannot remember a thing. I must have been in shock. When they arrived, they gave me a hollow green stick to suck on. This eased the pain, they cut my boot off and my good trousers. No arguments, hospital was where we were going. This was my first ever ride in an ambulance. Frankston Hospital got a guernsey again. My foot was at right angles, certainly not where it should have been. The surgeon looked at it and up to the operating theatre we went. They put the whole leg in plaster up to my thigh. Again, for the period that the ambulance pulled up at the hospital, it is all a blur. I only remember bits and pieces, plus the little green stick that you suck on also puts you out of it as well. That's what I put it all down to anyway. An unusual thing for me as I usually remember most things.

I was released after five days and was sent home. By golly! It was bloody hard to get around on crutches. The plaster on the leg weighed a ton. Like a twit that I am, I pushed for them to let me out before Christmas; no one wants to spend Christmas in the hospital. They let me out on Christmas eve. Very nice to be home in time for the celebrations. I do think they let me out too early, should have stayed in several more days because Christmas Day for me was excruciating. The pain was something I'd never gone through before—what they did, opened my knee, and put a titanium rod down through the knee to the ankle. The pain in my knee was absolutely wild. The hospital did not even give me any pain relief at all; the Panadol we had did nothing. Most doctors we called were not available as it was Christmas Day, and they were not interested in coming out.

My daughter finally got onto one. He came out, said "you, poor bastard, having to go through that without any pain relief." He gave us some Endone, and he was on his way. At least I was able to have some relief at long last; Christmas dinner was certainly much better without the pain. That would have had to have been the worst Christmas Day I have celebrated in all my life. Next time I will listen to doctors and take their advice and not fight them all the way as I did. I certainly paid the price for that.

Over the years, I have had my fair share of accidents and incidents, including two broken ankles which has caused some sort of grief and pain. Well, I tell you, this pain in my knee, not where the bloody leg broke but where they put that fucking rod, was the worst that I have ever been through. It affected the nerves around the knee and no matter what I took, there was no relief. For the first time ever, I cried with the pain, not ashamed. It just bloody hurt.

I had to go back to the hospital after three weeks so that they could check on the plaster and to see if the leg was healing. When they took the plaster off, the smell just about knocked us out. I did not know that when the leg broke, the bone broke the skin and that area had become infected. What the doctors were afraid of was if the infection had gone into the bone. If it has, there was a chance I could lose my leg. I spent most of the day having tests, checking how far the infection had spread. We had kicked a goal. The infection had not spread, thank God. They did not allow the plaster to go back on. The wound would not heal under it. Also, the wound will be a lot easier to treat without the plaster, so I had to get around on crutches without the plaster and the leg would take longer to heal because of this. And it did. "Shit happens."

We were told that the titanium rod could stay in the leg no longer than 12 months. After that time, it can get moulded to the leg and you would never get it out. At the time, we did not have a private hospital cover. Seeing that I am accident-prone, my doctor suggested that if I can afford the private health cover, I should get it because I will need it if I have any more sickness. Frankston Hospital also contacted me to put me on the waiting list for the rod removal. This all turned out to be a good move.

I had decided to register for private health, by doing this it would allow us a period of 12 months for any existing problems, you may have to be treated, so once I waited 12 months I could get the rod removed from my leg. I was told that the waiting list at Frankston hospital could be as long as two years. The 12 months passed and I was able to get the rod removed and paid for by the health fund. The unbelievable thing is that Frankston hospital contacted me 18 months later to say that my turn has come to have the rod removed. Turned out to be a smart move to get the private health insurance.

The wound on the leg had to be treated daily with a brand-new bandage each time, making sure that the infection did not get any worse. I took two courses of antibiotics that seemed to knock it on the head; the infection cleared up well after several weeks of treatment. I still had to treat the leg very carefully as it was still broken, and the breaks were taking quite a while to heal without the plaster.

At this stage, I was working for myself as a wholesaler selling goods to shops. I would buy products from the importer. He would appoint me as an agent to sell the goods on his behalf. The main product in the range were Toshiba batteries such as AA, AAA, C, D, 9 Volt. I was selling them to post offices which were independently owned. I could not service the corporate office as they were not interested in my product; they already stocked energisers which they were happy with. I had over 150 post offices as my clients which were serviced on a regular three-week cycle. I would walk into the shop, check the stands to see what they required. I would go and get it out of the car and deliver the stock immediately.

Each of them had a battery stand and if no one went to them, I would certainly lose business as there were many cowboys out there who would love to get more business by picking off my customers. They may not have had the same product as me, but they could offer them a similar product at a cheaper price. I had to be careful. Shopkeepers are only loyal to a certain point. My daughter took two weeks off work and agreed to drive me around and help out. I just had to show her where to go. She got the hang of it pretty quick. I was able to get the orders done successfully. All of my customers were happy. I explained that the next visit would be a little longer until my leg got better. After about eight weeks in all, I continued to call on my customers on crutches and get the orders that way. Most of my customers were quite happy to get the order themselves from the car and take it into the shop. It was a big hurdle that we got over. It is one of the very few times that my daughter Jackie was prepared to drop everything and help. Without her this time, I would have been in all sorts of bother.

The problem if you are self-employed is that the business is just good enough for one person to survive, hopefully without any mishaps. This mishap of mine is still very costly. I had to pay Jackie something for doing what she did for me; you can't take too much time from work to fill in for me without some reward. You cannot hire any outsider to do this work as they can get the idea of what you are doing, and they could try to start this sort of job up on their own. I did it; someone else could do it as easily. I have learned one thing: don't give anybody an unnecessary chance. In other words, don't trust anybody as they will try to bring you down. Anyway, we got by, and everything worked out well.

CHAPTER 2

From my knowledge, when you are admitted to a public hospital, you are assigned one specialist doctor to your case and you see him/her during your stay in hospital and after you come out in their private rooms. In my case, I was assigned a cardiologist named Buthandra. He was an Indian guy, a very large gentleman. All he did was interview you in his rooms, took your blood pressure and if necessary, he put you on a treadmill to do a stress test. If there was anything wrong, he would refer you to a cardiologist who did the procedures. I went to him for a period of 18 months; I felt this was a waste of time. If anything did go wrong, what could he do? So I asked my GP to refer me to another cardiologist, one that does the procedures himself.

My new cardiologist's name is Rodney. He operates at Peninsula Private Hospital, and his consulting rooms are in the same building. We won't use his surname as I have not had his permission to use his name in this book. The same will apply to any doctors' names that I refer to; only the first name will be used.

Over the years, I have had several heart attacks and have ended up in Peninsula Private Hospital, with Rodney doing the procedures. From memory, I think it would be at least four times that I went into that hospital and was treated by Rodney. He inserted stents each time he did the procedure. At least he keeps me alive. None of the attacks were large. I just felt murmurs in the chest, enough to get the cardiologist's attention. Each time he said, "Something is causing all this. It is better to be safe than sorry. Let's book you in." I was lucky that I worked for myself and had no problems taking the time off work. Each procedure was only one to two days off so really, it was no big deal.

Rodney has been trying for years to get me to give up smoking but like an idiot, I cannot see any dangers in it. I have seen all the advertisements relating to smoking and what damage the smokes cause the body but for some unknown reason, my brain does not seem to comprehend what happens. One thing I have learned is if you don't want to give up smoking, you never will. The body and the mind must want to give it up. At the time, we had private hospital insurance which enables us to go into private hospitals, and the insurance paid for the procedure. I certainly got my money's worth from them as each procedure cost between $5,000 and up to $30,000. I think I was the one who paid for the Mercedes Benz that Rodney drove.

I was getting older and every time I walked, my legs

began to have pain in the calves and thighs. My GP sent me to a vascular surgeon. I must explain what happened in the vascular surgeon's office. The initial vascular surgeon whom I made an appointment with was named George. Let's cut to the chase. I did all of the pre-appointment ultrasounds and all those and had an appointment at 2:30 on the Tuesday. I arrived early as I normally do at around 2 o'clock. I waited until 4:30 p.m.. I finally get in there to see him. His first reaction was not even a hello or an apology. He said, "I don't know what you're doing here. Looking at all the charts and the tests that you did, there's very little the matter with you." My immediate response was, "Well, why the bloody hell do to my legs ache?" "Jump on the table and we'll have a look at you." All he did was check my legs and said some calcification build-up in the arteries, causing a little blockage that it should be okay for a while before I need anything done. "I will see you in six months." What a waste of bloody time and what a pig. He certainly needed some counselling in his PR work. His receptionist asked me to book in for six months. My reply was, "Don't worry, darling. I won't be coming back." "Why?" "There is an old saying, 'you can get a grunt from a pig any day.' No, thanks." Peter, my GP, was told in no uncertain words: don't you ever send me to a pig like that again. What an arsehole. Peter thought I would get along with him, no thanks. He then referred me to a new vascular surgeon, Charlie.

It turned out that Charlie also insisted that before going to see him, he would insist on an ultrasound on the legs as well as do a stress test again to test the legs out. This became an annual event. First, the ultrasound. She would check out the arteries in the stomach and each leg down to the ankles. The stress test was next. She would check my arteries under normal circumstances and then onto the exercise bike for 15 minutes. She would then check the arteries under pressure. All the reports were sent to Charlie, and he knew what was going on with your legs when you got there; he would explain that this artery was 70% blocked and so on.

My biggest concern with my legs was if Charlie could no longer put stents into them, a bypass maybe necessary; most people would not be aware that a bypass could be done on the legs. The doctors remove an artery from each arm and insert it in each leg. What a mess—arms and legs all cut up. According to Charlie, it takes months to heal, and it is a very slow healing process. No, thanks, not for me if I can help it. I suppose I could consider myself fortunate that I missed a bullet.

My uncle Fred had bad artery problems in the legs but never the heart. He awoke one morning, and his legs gave way that he could not walk. An ambulance was called, and he saw a vascular surgeon at Frankston Hospital whose name was George. It turned out to be the same pig that saw me several months earlier; I gave him the flick before he could even touch me. The doctor opted for a full bypass, both legs. If they were my legs, I certainly would have questioned the doctor's decision. Surely to God, there would have been another alternative, but Fred went along with the flow. There were no questions asked and the surgery went ahead. This type of surgery keeps you bedridden for weeks, not being able to walk. It took Fred over four weeks before he could walk again and that was with crutches. He told me that the legs did not come good where he could walk pain-free for several years. If there was another option, I would have taken it. Nothing would have been as bad as what it was. I made sure that I did not see George as my vascular surgeon. I personally named him George the butcher which was kept between us. Never told him to his face.

For a period of around 10 years, I had problems with my heart and my arteries in the legs. Rodney could have performed a triple bypass which would have later alleviated all the procedures. I had to have stents put in every time I went into hospital. Naturally, he would get his fee and judging by some of the bills I got from Medibank, he certainly charged like a wounded bull.

Charlie would have operated on me at least three times over a period of 10 years. He inserted stents into my legs and the stomach where the veins go to each leg. I often wondered if some of these procedures were actually necessary; the legs did not seem to get any better once a stent was inserted. They seem to stay the same for years. I did learn later that if you have high cholesterol, the tablets you take can have an effect on the muscles in your legs, causing them to ache. I did go off the cholesterol tablets and found that my legs became better so technically, it was all one big waste of time. So, we will say at this stage that at least the operations seem to have worked as I have had no trouble with my legs for several years. Like Rodney, Charlie's procedures did not take long, normally a day for the procedure. Charlie was another one who was forever trying to get me to give up smoking without any success. He said, "I will have your legs if you keep smoking. I do at least three operations a year to chop someone's leg off. Don't let you be on the list so give it up." That did not seem to scare me enough to give the fags up. But something else did.

  Some things are sent to us to scare the hell out of us. I cannot remember exactly what day this happened, but this occurred. Say on Monday, I had a small twinge in my right hand where my fingers would not work. I was trying to pick something up without any success. I manipulated my fingers and the sensation had gone as quick as it had come. Two days later I was going to the toilet to have a wee. I went to pull out my old fella and I couldn't feel it. I knew it was small, but I didn't think it was that small. Again, my fingers went numb. I manipulated the fingers and it went away as quick as it came. I did not think much of this at the time. Early the next week in October 2010, I was standing in the kitchen talking to Jeanette and all of a sudden, my right arm went numb. What was happening to me? I could not move my arm. The whole arm felt like it was not joined to the rest of my body. It was not just the fingers this time. It turned out to be the whole arm. It just seemed to hang there. I started to manipulate my right arm with my left hand. As I was doing this, Jeanette was ringing the ambulance. The girl on the phone line was giving Jeanette instructions of what she should do. She told me I was having a stroke. I was starting to get relief by the manipulation I was doing, started to feel my arm and hands. The girl said to continue what I was doing; it seems to be working. She suggested that we cancel the ambulance and save them an unnecessary trip. The manipulation of the arm would have taken me over half an hour but eventually, everything came good as if nothing had happened. We rang the GP immediately and he suggested we ring our vascular surgeon as he was the person to see. Charlie organised an ultrasound immediately and the next day, I was to go and see him. He said, "What are your plans for tomorrow?" I said, "I am heading off to Geelong to do some calls." His answer was, "I don't think so, I will be making you first cab off the rank tomorrow morning as your carotid artery in your neck is 75% blocked. That is what has caused your stroke, not enough blood getting through to your brain. You are bloody lucky. You know, usually, a stroke this size normally causes two problems—either it kills you or you are a vegetable. Consider yourself very lucky. Not one part of your body has been affected. The right arm usually means problems on the left-hand side. Not one side effect has taken place. Your speech is still good." He also added, "I bet you will give up the cigarettes now." How right he was. I went into the hospital at 11:00 a.m. I had my last cigarette at five minutes to eleven. The surgery took over an hour. He unblocked the artery. It looked like my throat had been cut. They kept me in the high dependency ward so they could keep an eye on my breathing. After several days, I was allowed to go home; that was a stay in hospital I did not enjoy. The procedure was called a left carotid endarterectomy. I thought at this stage I certainly have had my fair share of blocked arteries and strokes. Where does it end? At least I'm still alive to tell the tale.

In the year 2011, we moved; we lived in Mount Martha where we had a large garden and the upkeep was getting too much to handle. We were the ones who bought the block from scratch and built our first house. We had been there for 36 years, and it started to deteriorate. After this time, it needed a lot of work. At the time we did not have the dollars to spend on the house, so we decided it was time to downsize. Property in Mount Martha was soaring in price, making it prohibitive to purchase in the same suburb. As far as downsizing it was not an option, so we had to go inland to get a suitable price.

We purchased a brand-new three-bedroom and two-bathroom unit in Hastings which is a half-hour drive from where we lived. A unit was handy as the kids had already left home. What was good was we had enough equity in the house to pay for the unit, and I have no money owing. We were able to do the garden, were also able to put blinds into the living area which meant the unit needed no more money spent on it. The unit appears small from the outside but when you get inside, the whole place seems to look larger. What I like about it the most is the open living area; the kitchen, the lounge room, and the dining room are all in one, with no walls to separate the rooms. It makes it just one large area. The kitchen has an island in the middle, and we use barstools around the island for there is enough room for six people to sit comfortably.

The outside area has enough room for a small vegetable patch and a lawn. I put in artificial lawn as the dogs kept weeing on it and killing it. Now I had nothing to mow, so I killed two birds with one stone. It made life easier for me.

One area which appealed to me was that there was little maintenance to do for a year. I don't think anything would have to be done for at least 10 years. I am not the greatest handyman in the land.

CHAPTER 3

I did say earlier that I sold batteries. When I would go into the store, I would check the customers' stand to see what product they required then go out to the van and bring in the order that they needed. I would fill the stand up by holding the batteries in one hand as they were carded, and I will deal them out like cards and fill the stand. Part of the deal we had with the customer was to fill the stand for them. This certainly did influence my hands as doing these six or seven times a day took its toll to your wrists.

In 2013, I had the day off due to a public holiday. I thoroughly enjoyed the relaxation which I had during the day. I said to the missus, "Gee, I really enjoyed today. I should do this more often." She said to me, "Do whatever you like. It is your own business. You do not answer to anybody. What are you going to do? Ask yourself for a doctor's certificate?" So I decided to have the next day off as well. I was sitting in the kitchen having a cup of tea and daydreaming. What I was actually doing was contemplating my future. I said to Jeanette, "Do you know that most men die at around the age of 80? I am 67 at this stage, that means I have 13 years left. I do not wish to be working much longer. I think it is about time I gave it away." I decided then and there that I will retire. The next day I contacted a business broker. He put the business on the market, and we sat back and waited. I felt that the business was worth something as we purchase product from an importer and resold it. My customers did not have the knowledge to be able to buy the product, or they did not have the time to contact someone else. But why would they look elsewhere if they were happy with the service I was giving? I was one of the very few wholesalers who put the product out on the stands for the customer—just part of the service I offered.

My actual supplier told me he had doubts that the business would be worth anything as he said anybody could approach an importer, buy product from them, and do what I am doing. All they have to do is approach many of my customers and offer them a cheaper price. He said he could do it himself and cut me out very easily, but because I know you and have been dealing with you for many years, I would not do that to you.

What I was counting on was the brand name and the customer base to give me something to sell. Somebody starting from scratch would have a hell of a time to build up the customer base of at least 150 calls. My supplier was quite happy to continue to supply anyone that purchased the business at the same price he was selling to me. He supplied the display stands that the batteries stood on, while the customer had our stand. They would have to buy the product from us, otherwise, they would have to forfeit the stand. Clever, really. While waiting for someone to buy the business, I went to every customer, made them sign a document to show the stand belonged to us. Everyone agreed to sign it. But it also assured the new buyer that the customers would stay loyal and will buy products from him as they did from me. The only reason they would change is if they did not get on with the new guy.

My customer base was changing daily. In the old days, all the independently owned post offices were owned by Australian personnel but lately, any that were sold were repurchased by the Chinese. They were prepared to pay a higher price for the business. Many Australian people were not prepared to pay an inflated price. I found it very hard to do business with them; they either wanted the goods for next to nothing or could buy off their own friends at a better price. Most of the products were sourced from China. It was very hard to keep the business. I was even bluffing them, saying they would lose the stand if they did not buy from us. That did not faze them at all. Many of them stuck with me as they wanted to feel their way and maybe because of my "charm."

What luck. After eight weeks, a Chinese gentleman

named Zi made an offer for the business. He was the only one who had made any offer at all. The broker suggested we look at his offer seriously as there were not too many people in the market to purchase this type of business; it will only appeal to a certain person. I think he was right. So I tried to up his price and get a little more from him, but he would not budge, so we accepted his offer. The terms included were I train his man for one cycle, which meant I would take him around with me for a period of three weeks. We called on every customer once so he had a crash course on how to sell batteries and other products. Every one of my customers seemed quite happy to deal with the new people. It is amazing how you think you have friends in the business but they turn out to be business acquaintances. Not one of them has contacted me since I left the trade. The trainee's name is John who had never sold a thing in his life. I told him this is going to be a crash course on how to introduce yourself and your products into stores that don't have it and also to supply the stores that do have it. There is going to be a lot to learn but don't worry, John. I know what I'm doing, and I will train you so you are ready in three weeks. By golly, was the course full-on. No rest for the wicked. I must admit John was a good pupil, took in everything that I told him; he did not miss a beat. He was more than capable and ready by the end of the three weeks. Once he went out on his own, not once did he ring me to ask how something was done. There is not only the selling side of it which he took in his stride, but there was all the further teaching of how to use the computer, how to invoice all goods, pricing in general product knowledge. I was quite proud of myself on the way that I taught him in such a short time, but I knew what I was doing as I had done many training courses for salespeople over the years. So we had a good teacher. I did not mention that I also stocked over 50 battery-associated products such as torches, ranging from small to large, as well as other bits and pieces that a post office could resell.

John and Zi came around to my house to pick up all the goods from our van and garage and transferred them to his vehicle. He did not buy my van, so God knows how he was going to sell it or how was he going to hire a van. He never indicated how he was going to do it, and he certainly did not want to pay my price for the van. I only saw Zi one other occasion when I had to give John a spare battery for the computer. I've seen John on several occasions. The business is still going to this day after about seven to eight years; I didn't think it'll last that long myself.

I was able to sell off the van quickly, so that it was not hanging about. I did not need it as we had ourselves a family sedan to get around in. I would have liked to keep the van as they are very handy but as things turned out, we owed money on the van, and we owed nothing on the sedan—

simple equation. So, after working all my life, I now joined the oldies set. Seeing there was no income, I applied for the old age pension and the seniors' card, and we were all set for our retirement. We did learn very quickly that if you are debt-free, you have a very good chance of surviving on the aged pension; luxuries such as private health insurance is not an option.

What we did not have was superannuation; running your own business was hard enough to make a quid, let alone put it away. We struggled big time as it was hard enough just to make a living so superannuation was not on our agenda. The only money we had that could be used as super was what we got for the business. At least it's better than a kick up the bum. So, retiring on a large sum was not the go. Holidays and cruises that we should have had did not exist.

As the years continued, in 2016, I was diagnosed with type 2 diabetes. I was a little overweight. My GP has treated the diabetes with tablets. They gave me all the equipment and gear to check my blood reading daily. I would prick my finger with a gadget shaped like a pen. You press the top and a little needle comes out at the other end and pricks your finger, drawing blood. You then get a special strip depending on the brand; mine was an Accu-Chek strip. One end is dipped into the blood, the other end is put into the Accu-Chek machine which gives you a blood reading.

The doctors want the reading to be under five. Mine never was; it is always around six and eight. Every now and then the reading is much higher. I never worry about this; it has not affected me in any way as the doctor's medication seems to keep the readings down low. If there is ever a problem with the readings, I just speak to the doctor, and he prescribes what is needed so all is good. They put me on to a dietitian who tried to control what I ate and drank that went over like a lead balloon to me, so I dismissed her very quickly. I took the stance. If the reading was out of control or getting too high, I would ask the doctor for the correct medication to lower the ratings. I never once relied on a diet to get the readings down. It seems unusual that most men around my age have been diagnosed with diabetes 2. Maybe the doctors have shares in the machines.

I suppose I can be grateful for small mercies. One is that I did not contract IBM while I was working. Imagine the hands, trying to get orders up out of the car when your hands don't work. Carrying them into the store I would have to have used a shopping trolley every time. I can be grateful this has happened after the business has been sold.

I have now been retired for close to five years. I am finding that my hands are starting to stiffen up and my fingers are harder to bend when making a fist. The GP has put it down to arthritis and the repetitious work that I used to do with the batteries. I thought that that was probably a fair diagnosis of what was happening. I would find myself also stumbling on uneven ground, totally unusual for me as I'm usually pretty good on my feet. When mentioning this to the GP, it seemed to go through to the keeper, probably thought I was pissed at the time, and nothing was done about it. Several months went by and the fingers on my left hand seemed to be getting worse, and I also had several more falls. Both concerned me so again, I mentioned it to the GP. This time he took it more seriously and ordered blood tests. The test showed that there was a problem in a couple of areas. He said I would have to go and see a specialist and have more tests done; he was certainly puzzled on what was going on. Before going to the specialist, Peter did some tests on my muscle tone and said there seemed to be some weakness in my arms and legs. I had been telling him this for God knows how long, and it just went through to the keeper. He did not pay overly a lot of attention to it. About time he did.

He sent me to a neurologist; he practised in Frankston and had an absolute lousy bedside manner. His name was Russell. He made me do tests on my forearms, hands, fingers, thighs, and legs. He felt that the muscle tone was more than deteriorating compared to someone normal. He had an idea of what was causing it but was not 100-percent sure. He referred me to a specialist at Monash Neurology in November 2018 and would book me in for a muscle biopsy. "We will know for certain after these tests are done."

While waiting for a position to come up at the Monash Hospital, I did notice weakness in my arms, hands, and legs. I was struggling to lift normal boxes. I did not think too much of it. My falls were becoming more frequent but mainly when the ground was uneven. Every bloody time I fell, I landed on my right knee. I was worried that I might break it. I was lucky that I did not fall forward and hit my head on anything. My right knee kept on giving way on me every now and then. The left did the same but mainly the right. This sort of thing never happened to me before. I was very anxious to get to the bottom of it. Each time I fell, the knees and toes would get grazed. Each time, the grazes took longer to heal. I would just about to heal a wound then I would get another. I tell you, we really stocked up on larger band-aids and gauze. Also, when you have diabetes 2, the healing process takes longer with the leg's feet and toes. You must take every precaution to stop any infection. Many diabetics lose their legs because of the lack of circulation in that area.

It was not only the knees and feet that copped the brunt of each fall. Many times, the arm would be put up to shield a fall. The back also cops a bit of a belting. I must admit I think the whole body hurts like buggary. I thank my guardian angel for keeping me away from the breaking area. If I break something, that is going to put me back a long way.

Also, I noticed that with each fall, it was taking me longer to get up and recover from it. I thought I was reasonably tough or strong, but I tell you with each fall, it is getting harder and harder to recover. I would lay on the ground longer and would try and assess the damage done. Eventually the body would say "come on let's move" and then I would struggle to get up. Sometimes it was bloody hard to even move. I will say it again: I am so lucky I did not break anything. At least that was on my side.

CHAPTER 4

Whilst continuing to wait for the biopsy, my GP did not have a clue what was going on; he could not give me any explanation as to why I was falling over and how my left hand was unable to make a fist. My right hand was not affected in any way. Finally, a date was set for me to go in and have the biopsy at Monash Neurological Department. It was set on the 18th of January 2019. It turned out it was a day procedure. I went in at 7 a.m. They administered a local anaesthetic to the area where they were going to take the biopsy. The surgeon then took a chunk out of my leg and sent it off to pathology for the results. It would take two weeks before the results of the biopsy would be known.

Russell, our lovely neurologist with the perfect bedside manner, contacted us to let us know that the results of the biopsy were in and for us to come in and see him so that he can give us the good news. He invited us to sit down and then delivered the news. He said, "The biopsy is conclusive with IBM (inclusion body myositis). It is a very rare disease especially in Australia where ten in a million people contract

IBM. (Those were his figures; it is actually higher.)

There is no cure. There is no treatment. Nothing will work with it. The doctors still have not come up with anything to cure it. You will just have to live with it. Normally there's no severe pain associated with IBM. For some parts of the body, you may require a mild pain killer. IBM is a disease which will attack all of the good muscles in the body especially the arms, hands, and the thighs. The disease is a slow progression, very similar to MND (motor neuron disease) but a lot slower. I would expect you to be in a wheelchair within 10 years unless the doctors are able to come up with some sort of cure. Exercise is recommended for the affected parts but only mild because if you overdo it, you will cause more harm. Once the muscle is dead, there is no comeback; it will stay dead. Any questions?

"WOW… you could have knocked me over with a feather. So much was said in such a short time, so much to take in." That's what I mean by his manner—straight out with it. He does not even give you time to catch breath. He said, "Naturally I will monitor your progress." The only question I had was what will happen to my body. Will this progress? Be fast or slow? What is going to happen to me? He said all cases are different; one person can be affected in their arms, another person in the legs. It is very rare where there are two same cases.

He did organise some physiotherapy at the local

rehabilitation centre and also some social help which certainly did come in handy for me.

That afternoon, we went and saw Peter, the local GP, and he was gobsmacked. In his 40 years of practise, this is the first case of IBM that he has encountered. "Looks like I will have to study up on this to find out what treatment I can give you if there is any. This disease is new to all of us." "Are there any medicine on the market which will the treat muscles, something to strengthen them?" Peter said, "There are vitamin tablets such as high-strength magnesium and Coenzyme Q10, 300gm a day. Both are good in helping the muscle tone. Also, you could try an all-purpose vitamin pill daily." Naturally, I was prepared to try anything, anything that could help even if it is in a minor way.

It would be interesting to see what the doctors could do to help me as I was noticing the total change in my body. I have never had thick legs, but they were losing muscle tone. When I walked and if the ground was uneven, if there was a twig or a small piece of wood, I had to be so careful if a tile was raised, and I stood on them "arse" over. I would go without any warning. I was having difficulty climbing stairs and ladders. This was happening gradually but certainly enough to keep me on my toes.

I probably first noticed a change in my hands around 12 months ago. The progression has been—from stiff fingers to not being able to make a fist in that period. My right hand is now starting to have signs of stiffening. Most people take it for granted; what they can do with their hands, they don't really think they just do it automatically. What I must do now is think ahead and plan accordingly. I am the chief cook and bottle washer; I have done all the cooking at home since I retired so this is going to be a big challenge for me to prepare the meals at home.

My daughter, Jackie, moved into a new double-story house in Cranborne South. She sent an invitation to visit and have a look at the new abode. I told her before we got there that I will have problems climbing the stairs as I just cannot do it. She said, "That will be okay, we will help you." To climb each step, I had to grab hold of the rail and pull myself up step by step. Going down was just as bloody bad. You have to be so careful. I did not fall luckily, but that is the last time that I will be climbing anybody's stairs. I was exhausted. Early days with the ladder I would have to pull myself up step by step. Now I cannot even get up the first step. Anything with a step forget it. It is a no-go zone. Both Jackie and my granddaughter, Kayla, hung onto me for dear life.

I was very grateful that we were living in Hastings in the new unit because if we had been in the old place, I would have been in big trouble. There were six stairs leading to the front door and at least another five leading up to the garage from the backyard. With me being unable to negotiate stairs, I would have been in all sorts of trouble. I was still able to climb stairs but with great difficulty. As I just mentioned in the last paragraph, going down was just as bad; if I went too fast, I would fall. Again, I would have to hang on for dear life to make sure I kept my balance. I was starting to have big problems with the step leading out from the lounge room to the backyard. It was like a double step; the sliding door added an extra step to the task and the number of times I stumbled trying to negotiate that step I most certainly lost count. I installed a half step just outside the door that eliminated anymore stumbles; the same problem occurred at the front door to a lesser degree. We had an OT (occupational therapist) assess the unit to see if we needed ramps and handles installed to assist the way we were able to move around. A rubber ramp was installed at the front and backdoor as well as handles to hang on to. The ramps and handles have eliminated any falls at the front and back door. I don't think my knees could have put up with much more.

Checking out Google to find out what information was available about IBM, there are certainly studies going on throughout the world. Although very small, at least something is getting done on the subject. Unfortunately, doctors do not even know how this starts. In Melbourne, Australia, there is a group called Myositis Association-Australia Inc. which I am now a member. The president's name is Christine Low. The website is www.myositis.org.au. We have had a couple of meetings of persons affected by IBM on the Mornington Peninsula. I went to two of the meetings and informed Christine that I won't be going to anymore as I was not getting anything out of the meeting. I was more advanced than any person. Also, not one of them had hand problems, so I could not see where I was heading, not that I really wanted to know. Rather scary, I think. Christine put me onto a guy who was in a wheelchair this time. It was too advanced for me. She has been excellent. No problem is too much trouble. If I'm feeling down at any time, I can get a lift by speaking to Christine. Also, her knowledge of IBM is second to none. As Russell said, there are no two people who have the same case, and it's very hard to compare notes.

The ramps at the front and back door were a godsend. I was able to walk more carefully thus avoiding the falls. But once I got outside, it was a different story. We have tiles under the pergola area in one section. They are lifting up which makes the ground unlevel. This one time, I stepped onto the raised tile and bang! My left knee went on me. When I fall, I fall forward slightly but not enough to cause any damage to my head. My legs and ankles take the brunt of the fall. Jesus did that hurt my knee and my ankles copped the lot. My big toe and the one next to it on my right foot felt as if it was broken or badly bruised.

It took me awhile. I just seem to lie there, get my bearings, and assess what damage has been done. I was able to get up and hobble inside with minimal damage. It certainly could have been worse.

As mentioned earlier my myositis was diagnosed in the year 2019. Prior to that date, I feel it was active possibly 12 months prior. Earlier, I mentioned Russell sent me to see a physiotherapist and concentrate exercises on the affected parts of my body, mainly the hands, arms, and thighs. Tests were done on the hands to see how much strength I had and how I could use them. What I did find interesting was that no physiotherapist had come across anyone with IBM. Both of my physiotherapists were concerned with my ability to hold the steering wheel while driving and how I did when turning the wheel. If I was having any problems at all and my ability to control the wheel was being impaired in any way, they would have to report it. You did not have to be Houdini to work out that I was lacking the ability to hold the steering wheel correctly, so my time left driving is limited. I will know when it is time to stop.

I was starting to look like I prisoner of war—all skin and bones with a pot. I was struggling to pick up a two-litre bottle of Coke. I could not pick up a chicken in one hand. Well, I've never had a big bum but now, it is skin and bone and I have to use a cushion to sit on to make it more comfortable. When I sit, it eliminates the skin and bone effect. If I don't use the cushion, my bum aches. My lift chair in the lounge and my bar stool at the island both have a cushion on each.

Found the exercises to be hard work where he said, do 50, we could only do 20. The instructor was very wary not to overdo it. I found the hand exercises near on impossible. All I could do was massage the fingers; it gave me relief for only a short period. It is just a waste of time. Instructor said there were very few exercises designed for the hands. They gave me the squeeze balls to help strengthen the hands by squeezing the ball. I did not have enough strength in my hands to even squeeze the ball. If you can't bend your fingers and make a fist, nothing seems to work. An area the physiotherapist worked on was the forearms. I was starting to have difficulty getting out of a chair. I would have to push my bum up with my arms. If the chair is too low, I could not get out. I continued the exercises for two months and found they did absolutely nothing. It did not matter what extra exercise I did; it did not put extra muscle tone on any part of the body. I said to the therapist that this is a total waste of time. My body is just getting worse. To give you an idea, I would do a set of exercises designed for the legs instead of helping it hindered, and my body would just ache. Both the therapist and I decided to give it the big A.

Also included in the programme from Russell was occupational therapy. They thought they may have some gadgets in their collection that could help my hands. I felt many of the gadgets were for people with worst disabilities than me. Maybe in the future, some of the products may come in handy. We will be able to go through many of the products. Further down the track we get introduced to another OT. What we will do is incorporate both OT ideas then have a chapter on them.

I found it was getting harder and harder to see my GP, Peter. I would ring the surgery, and this receptionist would say he is not available for at least a week. I said I want to see him now, not next week. Sorry I cannot do so. I decided to make a change. I contacted a doctor in Hastings called Bradley and transferred my details to him and away we went; he seemed quite a nice guy who seems to know what he was talking about. I explained about the IBM and naturally, he had not heard of it so I had to give him a crash course and what happens to the body. I decided to leave my prescriptions with Peter.

Explaining all the medications to Bradley was too much of a hassle to go through; it was easier to leave that part as it was.

I noticed that my diabetes reading in the morning were getting rather high. Normally they range between 6.9 and 8.5. This is a normal reading for me. Over a period of three weeks, the rating went from 8.5 up to 24.4. I mentioned this to Bradley. He did not seem to care. He said, "Oh, that's no problem." I had to see him three days later, and I had a reading as high as 27.1. These are his exact words: Are you still worried about that? I told you it is nothing to worry about. Make an appointment for next week and we will go through the numbers and change medication if necessary.

As it turned out I had made an appointment with Peter to organise some more scripts for the medication I was on. While visiting, I told him what the numbers were. Immediately he went into action, ordering a needle to administer insulin. He said, "You are an inch away from taking insulin on a daily basis. Very lucky that you came to see me as this could have gotten out of hand very easily." Guess what? I gave Doctor Bradley the big A. What a bloody clown. How can a doctor not care about your diabetes readings? Maybe I should have made him aware of what he was doing or what he was not doing in my case. I feel more guilty by not letting him know about it now than what I did at the time. Maybe I should drop him a friendly little note.

This finally gave me the opportunity to tell Peter that I was ready to make a change of doctors as he was very hard to see. It is sometimes more than a week before an appointment was available; the girls at the front desk did not think it necessary to contact him to let him know that there was a problem. He said, "The next time this occurs, leave a message for me to ring you so that we can sort it out that day." Unfortunately, Covid has hit us and that has changed the way we see the doctors. It has made it even harder to see him. Fortunately, all my medical problems seem to be under control at this stage; seeing a doctor is not overly important. My body seems to be plodding along just nicely without a doctor's assistance. Let's hope it stays that way for a while.

Jeanette and I have been seeing Peter for over 25 years. I found him to be a very caring doctor and was very accurate in most of his diagnosis especially for me. I thought he was a better man's doctor than a woman's doctor. Luckily, she had never had much matter with herself to warrant Peter's intervention. I have thought for many years that Peter is starting to get a little bit complacent. Many times, you would mention something, and it seemed unimportant or uninteresting for him to act on it. That is another reason why I was considering a change. I have not mentioned this to him, and I will just see how he performs in the next few months.

CHAPTER 5

I did not mention earlier that Jeanette was diagnosed with frontotemporal dementia. It is the name given to dementia when it is due to progressive damage to the frontal and/or temporal lobes of the brain. The right and left frontal lobes at the front of the brain are involved in mood, social behaviour, tension, judgement, planning and self-control. The above-mentioned dialogue had been taken from the Dementia Australia Newsletter so it must be right. She has also been diagnosed with short-term memory loss so when combined, it's a large enough disease on its own. Getting old has never worried me. I never thought in my wildest dreams that both of us would be struck down with what cards we have been dealt. Jeanette was diagnosed at the Peninsula Health Centre in Mornington. I did not know the place even existed, then I found out what they do for you there. Everything is there for you. A social worker was high on our agenda. We were told that we must register Jeanette under My Aged Care where later they can assess her. Once assessed, she will go on the waiting list for a government-funded Old Age package. They start at Level 1 and end up at Level 4; each package has so many hours dedicated to home help.

This was in 2017 and at that stage, I had not even been diagnosed. I did mention that Russell had organised some things for us, including a social worker. She also encouraged me to register with My Aged Care and be assessed by them even though IBM does not show early signs of being a debilitating disease. I have to be ready when the symptoms do occur, making sure My Aged Care is aware of the problem as well. After being assessed, you can wait for up to 12 months before it is approved. At this point, we have had Mornington Shire council send a person into the house once a fortnight to do the cleaning. Once you have a government package, that all changes; the council is given the flick and the package takes over. We then must appoint at my home and the community care company who will appoint a care manager. They then decide who and what will take place with the hours that have been provided to us in the package.

While you are working, you are not aware of what the government offers older people. I did not know that they want people to stay in their own home and not go into a nursing home. The cost of keeping a person home is a lot lower than having keep one in a nursing home. There are so many programmes out there to assist people like me without any knowledge to get into the know. I found out that there is a carer's assist programme which entitles the carer to $136 per fortnight, certainly better than a kick up the arse. Most of the forms are available through Centrelink online. Just pick the form you want fill out; some of them need a doctor's approval. Get the doctor to fill it out and then send it to them. There's even a programme for someone who is incontinent. The nappies or pull-ups are paid for by the government to the tune of $630 per year. Again, fill the form in, get your doctor to approve it, then send it in and Bob's your uncle. I felt that I didn't have to have a carer's allowance as I was caring for her anyway. People higher than me all said you may as well have it as some who are not entitled to it claim it anyway.

Twelve months have passed since the first diagnosis. I was due for another visit with our friend, Russell. He was his normal self, just an arrogant prick who decided that more tests were required. After they were done, he did say that my position was much worse than when we started. He felt the deterioration is more rapid than what he expected. Unfortunately, there's still no cure for your condition. You just have to plod along and deal with it as it comes. I felt in my mind he was correct. I have noticed that my thighs and arms have lost a lot of mass. Also, the fingers on my right hand are starting to catch up to the left hand. Areas that I'm starting to have trouble with is the dressing of oneself. I'm now finding it very difficult to do buttons and tie shoelaces. My pointing finger and my thumb do not join. Try to eat some peanuts with that scenario. Because of my finger and thumb not joining, I find it very hard to grab my trousers and pull them up. Also, the bath towel in the bathroom is becoming heavy, and I'm finding it hard to dry myself after a shower. Maybe it is time that we had a helper in to shower and dry me off.

Finally, Jeanette has had her Level 2 package from the government approved which means we can get rid of the council guy who comes in and cleans our house every two weeks—if you could say he cleans. I should say he makes an appearance every two weeks. Let's leave it at that. What we must do now is appoint a manager who then controls what happens with us, providing we have enough hours in the package. These guys are a dime a dozen; they have popped up out of nowhere. They take a fee for every service they offer and also get a slice of the pie when an hourly rate is concerned so they double dip. Several of our social workers have recommended companies which we can contact. As it turns out, my son's wife, Elsa, has a very good friend who works in that field. She turned out to be a case manager. Her name is Renee.

She explained to us that the Level 2 package entitles the bearer to 13 hours of care a week. To give you a break down, you could have two hours of cleaning per week and the rest can be taken up as respite care where the carer will sit with you, play games, or just keep you company. At the end of the month, if the money has not been used, it can be accumulated to purchase medical equipment. We appointed Sai as our homecare provider. A new rule has been bought in: if there is anything we require medically such as lift up chair, a hospital bed, or anything of that nature, just let Renee know and she will order it in for you. The product must be ordered through a registered medical supply company. In the short time I have been involved, I have found that so many people rort the system and get away with murder, upping their prices to a stupid price knowing that the government or NDIS will pay for the product. Many times, if the product I want is small, I will just buy it anyway and not worry about getting reimbursed through the system.

Several times, I have purchased a product through eBay, and I see they're not a registered medical supply company. I cannot claim the product back. For the money I saved, it is not worth claiming for anyway, too much stuffing around.

I must admit one thing: there is no joy in getting older. Most of our friends are either dead or around our age. Every single one of them has some type of ailment or under a doctor for something. The body just seems to wear out. My grandfather, Charlie, had so much the matter with him. The doctor said, "He was dead, but he would not lay down." And one peaceful night, he died in his sleep. What a way to go. I used to say the same about Nana. Her name is Olive. She took so many tablets in the morning. It is a wonder she did not rattle when she walked. Bless their souls. Now I am doing the same thing.

Jeanette had a weekend from hell. It all started on a Friday when she went to ground. Meaning, she went onto the floor and could not get up. I tried to lift her. Absolutely no hope with my lack of muscle tone. I was certainly pushing shit uphill. The only way around this was to call an ambulance. They arrived, and we learned that the paramedics are not allowed to physically lift a person to their feet or even to a sitting position as it would play havoc on their backs. They have what is called a lifting cushion which is made up of four flat cushions joined together like a Konstantina. Each cushion has a separate section they blow air into. They use a portable pump and they have the patient sit on the cushion and they gently blow up a section at the time which lifts the person up. The paramedics were able to lift her, and we were out of trouble. On Saturday morning, again, she went to ground. I called an ambulance. The receptionist again said that they are running behind, and this could be a couple of hours plus wait. I decided to ring Shane. He came over within half an hour and lifted her up. Much to my surprise, within two hours, she was on the floor again. She could not explain why she was going to ground. She was mixed up, disorientated, and it seemed as if she was walking around in a daze, not really knowing what was going on.

Shane was summoned once more and again, he came over and lifted her up. That evening, bugger me dead if she didn't go to ground again. Shane was unavailable, so the ambulance was called. One of the paramedics mentioned that there was a smell in her urine which indicated a urinary tract infection. Because when she was standing up, she seemed disorientated. Something was certainly causing this. What had happened was she went to ground in the bedroom. Naturally could not get up to go the toilet. She did what had to be done where she lays. A blessing in disguise as the paramedic was able to let us know what the problem was. Monday morning comes around and guess what, down she goes again. The ambulance was called once more and this time, they took her to Rosebud Hospital where they treated the urinary tract infection. They kept her for two days and then sent her home. We have learned that a urinary tract infection can cause people to do very strange things, and it's not an uncommon thing for what happened to Jeanette to occur. It really was the weekend from hell. I'm sure the ambulance people were getting sick of us. Let's hope we don't need to use them for a while. I still don't know for the life of me why she kept going to ground. On a normal day, she won't go to ground once. I certainly don't know what caused this and unfortunately, she can't give me an explanation because of the dementia. Even the ambulance people could not give me any reason or explanation as to why she kept going to ground. We will never know.

I feel the IBM goes along in spurts. It seems to slow down for a while and then speeds up again. My thighs have disappeared; this is causing me to be unstable when I stand. I have to be so careful when I walk and be very aware of what I'm doing. I'm having difficulty getting up from a chair. I must rock myself backward and forward and get some momentum before I can stand up. If the chair is too low, I can't get up, I have noticed at the doctor's surgery, the chairs are very low and I have difficulty getting up from them. We have bar stools around our kitchen bench. They seem to be okay as they are taller, but the lounge room chairs are far too low. We have decided to purchase two lift chairs which will enable us to get out of the chairs in the lounge room a lot easier. Anyone wants to buy a leather couch?

Speaking to our case manager, we were able to purchase one of the chairs through eBay and have them pay for it. The cost was $600 which turned out to be paid for from our package. The other chair was paid for by ourselves. We bought the second one for $450. It is now a breeze to get out of the chair. Our case manager said that would be the last thing we can buy through eBay; the rest will have to go through an approved medical supplier. The lift chairs through the medical supplier start at $1,600 for the same bloody thing. Who's ripping who off? I would prefer to pay a lower price and be out of pocket than to be ripped up by these bastards. All we must do now is get rid of the couch which is sitting in the garage gathering dust. I was coming back from the park one day after taking the dogs for a walk and saw two guys rummaging through some furniture on the side of the road. They were looking at a couch which was in very poor condition. I went over to them and said, "Hey. Are you guys looking for a couch?" which they replied "yes." I said that if they were willing to come up to my place, I have a three-seater leather couch for free. I gave them the address and that afternoon rolled up and loaded it onto the trailer. Was very happy to see the last of it. At least, it will get some further use.

My assessment through My Aged Care has finally been approved, and I have qualified for a Level 1 package. This will be official in approximately four to five months. They really move fast, don't they? So at least that's something to look forward to. I have noticed that my falls are becoming more frequent. The problem I'm having is getting up. I find my hands starting to become stiff and harder to position them to lift me up. I was in Aldi's the other day and without any warning, my leg went from under me and bang, down I went. A woman asked me if I needed help.

I said, "No thank you. I am fine. This is what happens when you get old." What else could I say? You don't want to have to explain to every person you see what IBM is. I was able to lift myself up by using one of the displays on the floor, rather embarrassing. You know you are falling but you can't do anything about it. You feel your knee go and you know in your own mind there was only one place to go and that is down. The only thing to be careful of is that you don't hurt yourself. So far, I have been lucky that I have not landed on my head. It is always been on my knees and legs which buckle up and go from under me and they cop the full weight of my body. I tell you what, it bloody hurts. My knees are continually getting grazed, as long as they don't get broken. If I end up with a broken leg or a broken hip, I'm going to be in all sorts of trouble.

Another day, I'm down at the leash-free area of the park, walking the dogs, not a care in the world. I'm walking along the path and you guessed it, both knees go on me at the same time again. I feel them go and you feel so helpless there is nothing you can do but go down. I landed on my knees. As usual, it hurt like hell. I crawled onto the grass and tried to get up. I used my hands to push me but to no avail. No matter what I tried, I just could not get up. There were two guys also walking along the path. One had one leg, and both came over to help me. They had no luck in lifting me. It must be just one big dead weight which makes it very hard for anybody to lift. I crawled over to a sign with the two guys' help. I was able to lever myself up the sign. Again, how embarrassing. It is bloody hard to get up when your legs, especially the thighs and your hands, don't work. I'm going to have to do something but what? Medically, there is nothing that can be done for the hands or the legs. I'm going to have to use a mobility walker at least, this should help me stand up and not fall as easily. Time will tell.

Jeanette already has a mobility walker at home which I used when I went down the park to take the dogs for their walk. What it did for me was give me the extra confidence I needed to stay upright. I did not care what people thought seeing this guy walking around with a mobility walker. All I cared about was staying upright. I got onto eBay and ordered a mobility walker for myself.

With the falls becoming more common, we decided to invest in a necklace which will detect the fall as it happens and will automatically ring the person you have nominated. It allows the person who wears it to have up to four people contacted when it detects a fall. Since I've had the little gadget, I have not had a fall while wearing it. We did test it out to see if it worked. I threw it to the ground. The sudden fast movement sent the machine into action. It immediately rang the first person on the list which turned out to be Shane. We did not tell him we were going to do the test and when the alarm rang, he panicked, thinking something had happened.

We assured him that everything was okay. He could not see the funny side of it, and I don't blame him. He said, "You have heard about the boy who cried wolf?" The little alarm is called Live Life. It operates on the Telstra network. The cost is $45 per year to keep the network active—well worth the cost. It only has to save you once to have paid for itself. The overall cost was around $500 which is the one-off purchase price for the actual unit and to have it operate on the Telstra 4G network. One morning at around 3 a.m., I heard my son calling out, "Dad, are you alright, Dad! Dad! Are you okay?" It turned out that the alarm, for some unknown reason, activated itself and automatically rang Shane. No doubt it was ready to ring the second person on the list before it could. We deactivated it. Naturally, again, my son thought that something was wrong.

At last, my mobility walker has arrived and now, when I walk the dog, I never go without the walker or my necklace. Most of my falls lately have been inside where I do not use the walker as it is not required. Maybe I should get used to using it inside and out so that I cover all areas.

CHAPTER 6

    I was notified by a woman called Lani who oversaw the social group at Hastings Community Centre. She also ran several carer's groups and asked me if I'd like to attend. Why not? It will get me out of the house and give me a break from Jeanette. The first meeting was held in Hastings, and there were six persons in the group. Everybody in turn was asked who they cared for and what problems they faced. Naturally, everybody faces different scenarios. Most of the carers had to deal with Alzheimer's or some form of dementia. After listening to everybody's problems, I thought I had it easy compared to them. I found it interesting to see how they dealt or didn't deal with it. The only problem was every month, the same group did not stay together. At least one or two of the participants dropped out so there were new people each month. Sometimes, only three or four would turn up. After a while, I found the meetings boring and repetitious. One thing you do get out of these meetings is how to claim things from the government. At this stage, I did not claim a carer's allowance. One of the guys in the group showed me how to do it online. Which I did, and then the payment was approved. Why not everyone else does it? The carers' group meet the first Wednesday of the month. It is in my diary, but I have not been for a while. We will see what happens in the future.

It has been 20 months since I was diagnosed with myositis. What a journey this has been. Never in my wildest dreams did I think I would have to deal with something like this. The progression has been relatively slow. Let's look at where we are up to at this stage. The hands cannot make a fist. I find that the forefinger and thumb can no longer join on my left hand. The right hand at this stage is nowhere near as bad as the left. The only difference in my physical condition is my upper legs. I've seen better legs on billiard tables. I'll have to think twice about wearing shorts this summer. The legs do not look good. I'm also finding it hard to lift things such as a two-litre bottle of Coke. I cannot lift it with one hand and have difficulty lifting it with two. I can no longer lift a slab of beer. I do not have the strength in both arms to pull weeds out of the garden, cannot use garden tools like shovel and spade, cannot turn the soil. I find it difficult to do the shopping. It is hard to pick things up out of your trolly when your hands don't work. I find it bloody amazing that no one offers to help you at the checkout. People stare at you and moan and groan that you're taking so long and holding them up but never an offer. One of the hardest things I find I must do is wipe my bum. This sounds funny, but I have not got the muscle tone in my hand to hold the toilet paper and push it to wipe. What I have to do at this stage is do the wiping as best as I can then stand over the bathroom sink and wash my bum every time I go to the loo.

With the packages that we both have—Jeanette on Level 2 and me on Level 1—our case manager found that by joining them together, we were able to utilise their services much better. At this stage, we have a lovely lady named Denise who initially came to us as a one-day-a-week cleaner. Shane came to visit one day when she was working. He said, "If she went any slower, she would stop. You are not getting value for money out of her." He spoke to SAI and had her removed. When we required one person to come in and spend time with Jeanette, she turned out to be the one. Lousy at cleaning but you could not get anyone better or as capable as she is to do this job. She is also qualified for personal health which means showering and dressing a client. She comes in two days a week in two two-hour shifts—one for Jeanette and one for me. She takes me shopping so any larger articles such as Coke or beer or a chicken, she's able to lift the products for me. I certainly do enjoy this time with Denise. We use my car as the one she has is very small. Every Wednesday morning, we make out a shopping list of what is required, do the shopping, come home, put it away, and then I have lunch. Each week, we take it in turns to shout the meal. Another lady named Rose comes in on a Wednesday for two and a half hours to do the cleaning. We find it better on a weekly basis as the house does not get as dirty. The package also allows us to have a window cleaner come in as required. This has been used once. Also, it allows us to have a gardener. He has come on a regular basis to trim the hedges and tidy up the garden in general. They seem to charge like wounded bulls. The last effort for two hours they charged us over $300. We will have to find somebody who does not charge as much. It usually takes two guys one hour to do the job. Talking about the package as we are, each has just been increased to another level by My Aged Care, making it Level 2 and 3. We must aim for a Level 4 for each of us.

Our friend doctor, Russell, has decided to retire. He was older than me not by much, only two years. He summoned me to his surgery for our last appointment together. He said, "There is nothing I can do for you. Nothing anyone can do for you unless doctors can find a miracle cure very soon. In 18 months, you have progressed faster than I envisaged. All I can do for you is wish you the best of luck." That was the last time I saw him. Certainly, no great loss; he did actually nothing for me over the period of the two years I knew him. He also charged like money was going out of fashion, as specialists do.

It was becoming a nuisance driving from Mornington to Hastings to see Peter. Also, I felt that he was becoming a little complacent with Jeanette and my ailments. It was all a little bit too hard, so we decided to change GPs. We chose a lovely English lady over at the Hastings Medical Clinic. Her name is Kelly. I sent a letter explaining to Peter that the drive is a little too much for us. It was easier to see a doctor over here. I never heard from him again. We are at the height of the pandemic, and it is becoming more difficult to see doctors.

Peter, prior to us giving him the flick, had referred us to our new neurologist. Her name is Deepa. All my history was sent to her, and an appointment was made. This girl was very nice-looking but absolutely as useless as tits on a bull in treating someone with IBM. she did not even examine me. Just looked at the file and said there is nothing that can be done unless a cure is found. Well, fuck me. I do not need to spend $150 and be told nothing can be done. My comment to her was, "I know there is no cure, so why do GPs continue to send us to specialists like yourself, when as you said yourself there is nothing you can do?" Her reply was, "I apologise to you as this occurs quite often, but in the future, if there is a cure found, you will need a specialist like myself to treat you. Also, if the condition gets too bad for you to handle, I am able to refer you to specialists higher than myself." I replied to her, "If this gets too bad in the future and I become a vegetable, I do not want to put up with that. If I'm in a wheelchair, I said I would need help from a hospital to deal with it." She referred me to an IBM specialist at Calvary Hospital where if the worst comes to the worst, they will help me out. I am now aware that the hospital has a palliative care unit.

As mentioned earlier, I had chosen a new GP at the Hastings Medical Clinic. Her name was Kelly, a rather large English lady with a lot of letters after her name. I had all my medical details sent out to her. I also told her about IBM; she was very interested to learn about it. She said, "I've never heard of it, but don't worry. I will learn as much as I can about it so we know what we're dealing with." She is at the same clinic as Bradley, the one that did not do anything about the high diabetic readings. Anyway, I don't think we will cross paths; we'll deal with it if we come to it.

CHAPTER 7

I mentioned earlier the things I can and cannot do, and one of the main ones was unable to wipe my bum. Having to go to the bathroom to wash my bum every time I use my bowels was becoming a bloody nuisance. Anyway, it is what it is. Now, it's certainly time to do something about it. I had heard of bidets in the past but had never used one, so I checked with Bunnings and surprise, surprise, they do not stock them. Why wouldn't one of the largest hardware and plumbing shops in the land does not stock this product? So, Doctor Google was used. I did not think there was such a range. It started from $100 for a basic unit up to $400 for the deluxe unit. Checked with the bidet shop and their prices started at $1,800 for the deluxe unit. It is the old scenario—claim it through My Aged Care and you can pay a premium price for the privilege. (Arseholes!)

So, I purchased two units one for each toilet—one for $380 and the other for $290. As I am a layman, I know nothing about plumbing. I learned later that the unit must have an Australian compliance certificate to be fitted by a plumber here. Guess what! No compliance certificates, so no plumber will touch it. If he fits something and is found out, he could lose his licence. Doesn't rain but it pours. This is also why the bidet shop charged a higher price since they come with a certificate. Denise, one of our carers, saw the box sitting in the spare room and asked why we had not put it together. I explained to her why. She said, "Let's give it a go." She followed the instructions to the letter. After two and a half hours, the bidet was working, but the water would not turn off. The cistern has a cut off valve, and this was out of plumb. Called in a plumber and what he did was legal as all he had to do was fix the cistern.

While he was there, I asked him if he would have a look at the other one. He explained what the compliance was about and how he could lose his licence if found out. So I suggested that he will supervise and I do it, which I couldn't anyway because of my hands. He knew exactly where I was coming from. I said, "He would be paid in cash and all you bill me for is a broken cistern." We understood each other beautifully. I knew that there would be no comeback if the bidet stuffed up. Thank goodness, the carer stuck her big nose in so in one day, we went from no bidets to two working bidets. I have not explained how they work—very simple, very practical. You have a toilet seat with some very nice extras. One is a seat warmer. You can have the seat warmed so that on a cold day, you end up with a warm bum.

There are two washing devices, one for both the male and the female, which is used for the rear end. You can adjust the water temperature to your own liking—warm, cold, or hot—and one for the girls which is used for the front end. After the water device is used, you then use the drying device which blow-dries the area. The dryer also acts as a deodoriser, taking away any odours which may occur in the bowl. My first time, I was very cautious, not knowing what to expect. I tell you, it is heaven. After I do the deed, press the remote, and a lovely warm gush of water sprays my bot. After that is done, I press another button and warm breeze dries the offender. No home should be without one. How dare you ask someone to use a normal toilet after using a bidet. With Jeanette's dementia, she forgets what buttons to push so it never gets used; mine is exactly the opposite.

My best mate, Phil, is an industrial chemist and manufactures many products like shampoo, conditioner, and many health-related products. He has people on his books that require him to make certain goods for them. One of his regular clients gave him a recipe and formula for an untried muscle building product. He wanted X amount made so he could send it to the USA to bodybuilding gyms. Many bodybuilders use this product to help build up muscles. It comes in a liquid form to be taken orally, one milligram a day. After putting this product together, Phil thought this could help Wayne. The cost of the finished product turned out to be around $2 a milligram. It tastes revolting, but I'm prepared to give anything a go which may help me in the long-term. The problem is, I am taking it but I don't know if it works. Maybe if I go off it and there are changes, I will know. The name of the product is Osterine, another name is Embosom. If you Google either of the names, the following is what it says: Embosom, also known as Osterine, is an investigational selective androgen receptor modulator developed by GTX Inc. for the treatment of conditions such as muscle wasting and osteoporosis. At this stage, it is not approved by the FDA, but it is sometimes found in supplements. I've since learned the reason Phil was asked to manufacture the product here was that it is illegal to manufacture the product in the USA without a medical certificate. I've learned one thing: ask no questions and you will be told no lies. Let's leave it at that.

It is now the 11th of January 2021. The time is 1:50 a.m. I'm awoken by a pain in my chest. I thought to myself at the time, "been there done that." This will pass, no problems. So I sat up on the side of the bed thinking that this will go away shortly, but the pain continued. As I said once before, it is like having a clamp on your chest. At 2:00 a.m., there was still no relief. I thought "I'm in trouble here, I think I'd better call an ambulance." They were called at 2:05 a.m., and I explained that I've had heart attacks before and I knew exactly what it was. While they were dispatching an ambulance, I rang

Shane. No answer so I left a message, explaining what was happening. I rang my grandson Clayton and told him "not to panic, I'm having a heart attack, and to let your father know so that he can come over." I think he was half asleep as he did not really comprehend what was happening. Within a couple of minutes, Shane rang. Clay gave him the message. Shane explained that he never has the phone on silent, but that night, he decided to charge it, that is why he could not answer. At 2:20 a.m., believe it or not, I'm still having pains. I've never had a heart attack last so long. The ambulance paramedics arrived at 2:30 a.m. Shane arrived just after. I explained to them how long the pain had lasted and had never had a heart attack last as long as this. I sat next to the kitchen bench on one of the bar stools. They did an ECG and confirmed that I was having an attack. The pain was not constant; it did enable you to catch your breath, but really I felt like shit. The pain had really eased now; what the paramedics were doing was certainly working. It had given me some relief, thank God. It is getting close to 3:00 a.m, and the pain has finally eased. From start to finish, it lasted close to an hour. If it was going to kill you, you would want it to go faster than that. Two more paramedics arrived when the first group confirmed it was a cardiac arrest and when that happens, they need an extra two paramedics on the scene. I still have not found out why. I think it's a waste of resources where the other two could have been doing another job. Off to Frankston Hospital I went, straight into the cardiac arrest ward where the doctors hoped that it could be cleared up straight away. They performed an angiogram, thinking that maybe a stent would do the trick, but not to be. He said there were too many arteries blocked. I would need a triple bypass, and they decided to send me to the Alfred Hospital that morning.

The same ambulance which brought me to Frankston took me into Alfred Hospital. It certainly tied the ambulance up for several hours. It felt like an eternity that I was in emergency, but it was only a couple of hours before they admitted me into a ward. The doctors' main concern was that my heart was racing at a faster rate than normal. The number of doctors and students giving me attention was annoying, but they're only doing their job. The best place to learn is the practical side on the job. No one in the cardiology ward that I spoke to had ever heard of or seen anyone with IBM—totally new to them. The doctors finally got the heart rate down. I heard one of the cardiologists say, "Keep an eye on this one, it could blow up at any occasion."

I was in a ward with three other guys; the other three all had heart problems. Naturally, we are in the cardiology ward ha. If you are going to have a heart attack, this is the place to be. After the second day, I was feeling pretty ordinary. One morning when I said to the nurse, "Oh, oh. I'm getting pains in the chest. I think I'm having an attack." Well, all hell broke loose. There were doctors and nurses coming from every direction. I certainly was the centre of attention. I could not remember everything they were doing to me. All they wanted to do was get my heart rate down. Again, they finally did. Boy, oh boy, was that hectic. The nurse said, "Thank God, we thought we were going to lose you." so it must have been touch and go (certainly bloody scary). During the first week, my stay at Alfred produced two heart attacks in all. They finally got the medication correct. It seemed like it was trial and error. If one thing didn't work, they tried another.

The head cardiologist doing his rounds finally sat down and had a talk to me. This was what he had to say, "Sorry, we have mucked you around, but your heart has been so unstable that we could not do anything else until we got the medication right. You are booked in for a triple bypass the day after tomorrow. The head surgeon will come around and have a talk to you." That was the first time that they had mentioned a triple bypass, and the only time I had heard it prior to this was at Frankston. I certainly was not looking forward to this, not at all. The next day, the head surgeon came around and paid me a visit. You will love this. These were his words (I don't even know his name): Oh my God, where are your arms? Where are your legs? You are so skinny. You are all skin and bones. Do you have a medical condition we do not know about?" I mentioned IBM. Again, another one who did not know a fuck about it. I said, "It is a disease which attacks the muscles and leaves you like the way I am—skin and bones." His answer to me and to the other cardiologist in the room was: this guy cannot have a triple bypass. He will not get off the table; he is too frail. We must come up with another solution. We will get back to you this afternoon. I was quite happy to hear that. I did not want a triple bypass. Maybe I did kick a goal after all. I know I get annoyed when I find a specialist that does not know anything about IBM. I have been told there are over 7,000 diseases which have no cure. You cannot really expect every doctor to know every disease. Even so, it is still bloody annoying.

That afternoon, the cardiologist said they had a meeting just to discuss me. The only thing they can do for me is angioplasty and stents, and this will take place tomorrow afternoon. I laid there, a very happy boy; a bypass was the last thing I wanted to happen to me and now I got my wish. I had several doctors come over to me just to discuss IBM; the only one who would have heard of this is the neurologist at the hospital. None of them came to see me. There was talk that a neurologist was going to come and have a chat with me, but he never arrived, and I was ready to go home a few days later.

Well, tomorrow had come around. They prepared

me for the procedure and while in there, the doctor did two stents and one angioplasty which is clearing a blocked artery. He did say I had two other arteries blocked which they cannot get to at this stage because they're in an awkward position. It looks like I will have to have another procedure another time. Two days later, after spending 14 days in the Alfred, after making the appropriate appointments with cardiologists outside the hospital, I was allowed to go home. They actually sent me back to Frankston Hospital; I stayed overnight and was allowed to go home the next day.

It is marvellous what you learn about your family when an emergency occurs. Shane took two weeks off of work and stayed at my place for two weeks, supporting his mother and the animals. He prepared everything—all meals in between coming into the Alfred to visit me. What a star. He now takes me to all appointments and said he has to be hands-on, and he is there for me from now on.

The doctors at the Alfred say I must see my cardiologist or the cardiologist they recommend in four to six weeks. Why would I want to see one of their cardiologists when I could see Rodney, my usual guy? I went and saw Rodney exactly four weeks after I got out of the Alfred. To my total surprise, he had no paperwork of any procedure which was done at the Alfred. Either the Alfred stuffed up or Rodney's office stuffed up. We will never know. It just so happened that I had a total copy with me just in case he needed it.

He very quickly looked at it and said, "Why didn't they do the triple bypass? That would have been much better for everyone especially you." I explained why they did not go ahead with it, and he said they should have done it. Anyway, he did not seem overly interested in the case at all and could not wait to get me out of the door. Guess what, Rodney treated me like that, and I won't come back. He used to be good. I think success has gone to his head. All he seems to be interested in is seeing as many patients as he can. They are like cattle. If you have an appointment for 11:00 a.m., you will be lucky to seen by 12 o'clock. Every 10 minutes, people go in and out.

As it turned out, I checked the appointment that the Alfred had made with their cardiologist, and it was two weeks away so I kept it. The doctor's name is Nay Htun. I am glad I kept this appointment. It turned out that Nay was the doctor who performed the procedure at Frankston the morning I was admitted; he was the one who suggested I have a triple bypass and not to do anything that morning. He also works as one of the cardiologists at the Alfred. I certainly had made the right decision, giving Rodney the flick and seeing this guy. His knowledge of my case was outstanding, seeing that he was the first one to see me that night. He was very concerned that they were unable to unblock all the arteries and that another procedure should be done ASAP. As it stands, I am a walking time bomb and could have an attack at any time. An appointment was made at the Alfred Hospital for a day procedure at the cardiology general on 26th of July 2021. So here we go again.

Unfortunately, Nay was unable to do the procedure that day but assured me that his colleagues would be told to look after this special patient. He would drop in during the procedure but could not participate. Over the years, I have had many angioplasties. It usually takes a good hour, maybe a little more. This one took close to two and a half hours The doctors put in three stents and did angioplasty on no fewer than four arteries. Now I know what Nay meant by looking after this special patient. I did see him during the procedure, and we had a very brief chat. I most certainly hope that this is the last time that we have problems with the old ticker. When I say I am lucky, I mean fancy having a cardiologist who is one of the main heart people to operate at the Alfred Hospital. I just hope that Nay does not turn out to be like Rodney. He seems now only to be interested in the money. The more patients he sees in a day, the more money he makes. Surprisingly, he does bulk bill, which explains why he wants to push patients in and out of the door.

Let me explain what bulk bill means. Through our medical system here called Medicare, the government will pay a standard fee for a consultation by a specialist. The specialist for example may charge $200 a visit. The government, on the other hand, may only pay $100 for the same visit. The doctor has two choices: he can charge the patient $100 for visit and that gets paid to him by the government, or he charges the $200 and the government will pay the patient $100. Rodney still gets the $200.

So by bulk billing and pushing the patients through every 10 minutes so that works out at six patients per hour (let's have an hour off for lunch), they can still work till 5 p.m. and start at 8 a.m. That is 8 hours, 6 per hour, that is 48 per day. Not bad at $100; a pop be very hard to survive on $4,800 per day. Anyway, that's his choice; he does not seem to be short of patients.

CHAPTER 8

As mentioned earlier, Deepa, the neurologist, had referred us to Calvary Hospital where they specialise in IBM. I had three appointments on the day one with a neurologist, an occupational therapist, and a physiotherapist. They wanted to see how far the IBM had advanced since I was first diagnosed. Earlier, one of the nurses contacted me, asking who my first neurologist was so they could contact him and get all the records that they had on me. So, they were prepared when Shane and I walked in. The doctor's name is Mahi Jasinarachchi. I do not normally use their surname, but I had to. In this case, it was so short, not one you will remember easily. She conducted all the usual tests on my legs and hands and of course the arms. She said, "You are not as bad as some people that come in here with IBM. You are advanced, but you have a long way to go. I will see you in 12 months and do another "check-up." Gee, I thought if I'm not as bad as some people, God only knows what they are like. It gives me something to look forward to in the future. (Yeah, like hell it does).

The next one on the list was the physiotherapist. Unfortunately, she did not have a lot to offer because with IBM, once the muscle has gone, it is gone and cannot be revived. Also, you cannot overdo the exercises as it causes more pain than what it is worth. So really, we're stuck. She showed me several minor exercises, and it was left up to me whether I do them or not. I found that any exercise caused me grief, and I chose not to do them. "Que Sera."

Occupational therapist is on the list; we went through all the gadgets that may be required and used in the future. My hands are getting worse, but I'm still able to do things in the kitchen. When I'm unable to do that, that is when I will get some of the gadgets that I may need. One of the areas we discussed in detail was toileting. I was finding it hard to get myself off the toilet, so they looked at what options were available. This area has concerned me for quite a while. I have noticed that the frame that I use on my toilet does not seem to work as it should; it is not allowing me to get up easy. The normal frame sits around the toilet with raised arms which allows you to push up. I notice that I have no strength in my arms to push up so I'm using the back of the frame to push me forward as my arms are becoming weaker. I find it harder to do. There have been several occasions where I had to go to ground as I could not get off the toilet. Once I go to ground, I find it a challenge to get up. The OT suggested a toilet lift. She said she will check on the internet to see what is available and then get back to me. With anything we look at, we must be aware that the bidet must fit on whatever we get. Otherwise, it will not work. We bypassed several products because of this. We hired a new OT. His name is Mitch, and he works outside of Calvary Hospital. He can visit us any time whereas the hospital girl is unable to leave the hospital.

I have searched the internet high and low for some type of toilet seat that would be easy to get off. Over the years, there have been many on the market, but for some unknown reason, they don't last long. No sooner do they come onto the market then suddenly, they're off. I have found that the majority of these products are manufactured overseas, and it needs an agent to market the product in Australia. If the sales are not there or they do not have the money to market the product because without the marketing and letting people know what they're about, there are no sales, so I think the product is very limited in sales. I think the demand can still be high. Surely to God, this product would be in high demand. Well, I'm not the only one out there suffering from not being able to get off the toilet. Most of the products available are add-ons, such as a piece which goes on to the toilet seat, making it higher. That is not what I am after. We have finally found a company in Australia who are importing the product known as Lift a Seat. It is made in the USA which comes with an Australian price tag of $6,000. If you require something like this and you want it paid for by your package, first, you need an OT to recommend this product or any product for that matter. It must be written in your assessment that this product is required. Then and only then will the package pay for it, provided you have enough funds. Otherwise, you'll have to pay for it privately.

We had Mitch, our OT, organise the company to bring out a sample for us to try. There are two models: one that tilts and one that doesn't. We tried them both and settled on the one that tilted, so an order was placed and $6,000 was paid up front. How they work: it is a frame that fits over the existing toilet. It is made of stainless steel which is reasonably light. It has its own toilet seat which also enables you to fit a bidet. It has a remote control which has three functions—up, down, and tilt. You are sitting on the toilet and when you want to use the system, grab the remote, press up, and the toilet seat gets lifted. And when you are high enough, it will tilt; the tilt is slight so that you don't fall arse over turkey.

Very exciting time. Can't wait for it to be installed. It is going to be great to be able to get off the dunny like a normal person. Over two weeks had passed, and we had not heard a thing. I spoke to Renee, our case manager, to find out what happened to it. She rang the company and guess what? They are out stock. I was ropable. How dare they. Renee knew I was shitty and told me not to contact them. She was right. I was not happy, and I would have ripped pieces off anyone that I had spoken to that day. As it turned out, the representative rang me the next day, full of apologies. I had calmed down by then but also gave her a serve as I said to her, "We are relying on this thing. How dare you take the money when the product is not available? How long will the product be?" She said, "It is on the water and could be two to three months." She also said the product cannot be purchased from anybody else, so we have no choice. If we want that product, we just have to wait as they have several clients waiting. My answer to her was: you are lucky that you are the only ones that have it. As if you were not, you would not have my order. End of conversation. She could not have cared less. Nothing would give me the greatest pleasure than to cancel that order.

I had to come up with something. As Denise said to me, there is something so simple. It is staring at us in the face, and we cannot see it. How the mind works, some sort of hoist that can lift me up. She said, "What about one of those electric hoists used in engineering? Should be able to get one small enough to do the job. Let's give it a go." EBay to the rescue. I ordered two electric hoists. Why two? Honestly, I don't know why as I only needed one. Each time I see the spare in the garage, I shake my head; maybe we will use it one day. The hoist has a lift capacity of 150kg, plenty to spare there. It has a 3-mm wire rope. Will have to stop that from digging into flesh, could cause big damage if not handled correctly. If the wire can be connected to a leather sling which wraps under the armpits, the wire would not have to touch the body. Much of these ideas are in the mind, turning them into reality is the challenge. My OT shuddered when I told him my idea. If it is safe, that was all he said. I have since found out that if whatever it is that has been safety approved by the medical board, it is fine. If not, just forget it.

There are many leather slings on the market; finding one that can be utilized with my hoist is the problem. Basic slings start at over $100 plus, but many are not suitable. Found one on Kogan.com. Looks ideal and only $35. Only a couple of adjustments need to be made. When it arrived, Shane took it away and had several things done to it, like sewing a couple of hooks into it which will allow for the hook on the hoist to marry up with those hooks. The sling, when finished, looked the part. I wanted the hoist to be inconspicuous so not to grab attention, technically out of sight. Now, all we must do is find someone to do this job. The hoist would somehow have to be placed above the toilet door. There is a space between the door and the ceiling which could be used. The ideas are in the head; to make them into reality is the challenge.

My hands, being the way they are, there is no way I could do anything. I could not even lift the hoist; it was so heavy for me. So, in came a part-time carpenter. He connected the hoist above the toilet door, strengthened where the hoist was going to be so that when in use, the weight would not rip the arse out of the top off the door. It felt like the whole neighbourhood was there, ready for me to be lifted by this hoist. We placed the leather sling under my armpits, and Shane started it up and away it went. It lifted me, but I did not want to be lifted. I wanted to be pulled so the bloody thing lifted me in the air. Here I am, dangling with my legs all over the place. It felt awful. What do I do? For Christ's sake, let me down. And with my legs being the way they are, I felt very unstable trying to find my footing and as I panicked, everyone could see the fear on my face. Mate, just let me down. What a bloody disaster. As I said, I wanted to be pulled off the toilet, not lifted off. The way the hoist was set was too high, and you could not get it any lower anyway.

I was so disappointed that this did not work. The concept seemed so simple, but unfortunately, the host could not be placed on the angle which we needed for it to pull me off the seat. Everything worked fine; the speed that it lifted me was fine. Not being used to it caused a panic because once my legs are off the ground for some reason, I tend to panic. I seem to like my feet firmly on the ground... So back to square one.

The hoist could be used in another way and that is

if you were to build an A-frame made out of aluminium. It has to be light on wheels with the hoist sitting on the top. It could be used to lift a person who is on the ground. Any medical-lifting machines are large and cumbersome. This one has possibilities. All I need is someone to make it for me. I have not been able to convince anybody that this could work anyway. You must have an imagination to make things work in this world.

CHAPTER 9

We are now entering the two-and-a-half-year mark since IBM was diagnosed. I do feel it is increasing in pace. My right hand is catching up to the left—both becoming stiffer, fingers just do not bend, making life very difficult indeed. I am finding it much harder to do kitchen duties; even picking up a plate is becoming daunting. Two plates, no way, only one at a time. Surprisingly, my thumbs are not affected. I can move them any which way. Handling utensils is a challenge; large kitchen knives are getting harder to handle and naturally harder to cut anything you want, like dicing an onion. What a job. Pieces you cut end up in all different sizes and not what you want. I can still cut lettuce and tomatoes but anything that must be cut fine? Forget it. I cannot do it. Stupid things like picking up tomatoes. I find it very hard to hold them in my hand as your fingers control where the tomato sits; if your fingers don't work, the tomato goes wherever it wants to go. Anything I do anywhere and not just the kitchen now takes thought. I must think about what I am doing, so that I don't cause a catastrophe by injuring myself in some way.

The toilet scenario was starting to get a little bit critical as on three occasions in four days, I could not get off the loo. Each occasion, I went to ground and when this happens, I have to crawl out of the toilet into my bedroom and try to climb up onto a box I have at the end of my bed. This box is used to help the dog jump up onto the bed. I am starting to lose more muscle mass in my upper arms. I'm finding it very hard to push myself off a seat. When a bodybuilder or anyone in that fact flexes the muscles in the arms, you see a lovely big bulge take place. If I do that, the arm stays the same. No bulge, no nothing; the muscles just do not exist.

On one of our toilets, we have a frame with a toilet seat on the top. This seat is higher than the normal seat. I thought if I can take that seat off the frame and remove the bidet from our normal toilet and put the bidet on the frame, this might be able to overcome our problems. Jeanette uses the frame on her toilet, so we had a new frame delivered by our local mobility shop, and we put the idea into action. Guess what, the bidet fitted onto the top of the frame. By drilling two holes, we put the frame up to its highest level and sat. I was ecstatic. I was able to get off as easy as pie. It was a little high so we lowered it two inches. We might need those two inches later and now, I have a toilet I can get off, and it didn't cost me $6,000. What it did cost was $129. Unfortunately, we had the unenviable task of cancelling the $6,000 toilet. How sad. This little job of cancelling gave me a very satisfying moment—serves them right. Even the case manager it gave her great pleasure to let them know we wanted our money back. As we said, this was staring at us in the face, and we could not see it. And it is so simple. I don't know why we did not think of this earlier. The thing that got in the way all the time was the bidet. We needed something to work, and the bidet seemed to get in the way with every idea we had. As it has turned out, it was as easy as pie. At long last, the toilet saga has gone away. Hooray... I sent two emails with photo attachments—one to Renee, our case manager, and one to Mitch, our OT. Both were impressed. I don't think Mitch was overly happy about cancelling the expensive loo. Maybe he was getting a sling, I don't know.

A newsletter was sent to me by the myositis association regarding why people with IBM fall. What they were doing was promoting knee braces. I don't think they would mind too much if I was to steal a couple of paragraphs from the newsletter, which will explain it all.

For many people living with inclusion body myositis or IBM, falls are an all-too-common consequent of the disease. A study in the UK in 2014 reported that 98% of people with IBM had fallen in the previous year. For those over 65 years of age, it was 100%. Whilst many of these falls didn't result in serious injury, 5% of those in the study had a fall that required hospital attention. Locally, a survey conducted last year by our team found that 73% all myositis people had fallen in the previous year. This is much higher than the rate of falls in people without muscles disease.

Whilst no two people with IBM have the same patterns of disease, it is known that the weakness in the quadriceps muscles is the most common problem faced. The quadriceps muscle, as its name suggests, is a group of four muscles that combined to straighten the knee and to allow it to bend slowly under load, e.g., going downstairs. Of the four muscles of the quadriceps, it is the two muscles at the side of the thigh and knee that are affected most in IBM. It is weakness in this muscle that explains why many people with IBM can't straighten their knee fully.

The act of walking is a subconscious activity. As humans, even if we try to concentrate on what we are doing whilst walking, our mind will wander to other things, known as dual tasking. It is the ability to be thinking of one thing whilst doing another. We often tell patients in the Perth clinic that if they concentrate 100% of the time on their walking, they will rarely fall. For people with IBM, the most common mechanism of a fall is the knee "giving way." This occurs when the weight is on the leg when not fully straight.

Even with very weak muscles, if the knee is fully straightened, it won't give way. However, if it is just a few degrees off from full extension, it can collapse due to the weakness in the quadriceps. For people without muscle disease, if their weight bear on a knee that is not fully straight, they have enough strength to stop it from giving way. Clearly, Groucho Marx didn't have IBM!

Once the quadriceps muscle becomes very weak, it cannot fully control the knee as he goes into extension. For a number of Biers, the knee goes into extension with a considerable force that can't be controlled due to their muscle weakness. Often, when this happens, the knee becomes hyperextended, i.e., it goes back further than it should. For those AFL followers, this is a common complaint experienced by ruckman when they land on one leg and the knee is forced back suddenly and without control. Some patients do not experience pain when the knee is hyperextended considerably, but for others, it can be very painful experience.

For people without IBM or other forms of neuromuscular disease, the first approach is always to strengthen the quadriceps muscle via exercise. For those with IBM, whilst maintaining as much strength as possible in these muscles is vital, exercise alone will not provide the full benefits that those without muscle disease enjoy. Sadly, despite best efforts, people with IBM cannot fully reverse the weakness in their quadriceps with exercise alone. One option worth considering is a knee brace. There are many different braces on the market but not all are suitable for people with IBM.

The brochure continues with recommendations of what leg braces could be suitable. I won't go on anymore with what is written in the brochure as it does not seem applicable to me.

There are two areas which I have benefited because of this brochure. I totally agree with concentrating on what you do when you are walking. You do not think about what you are doing, your mind wanders elsewhere. Now, every step I take I'm thinking of what I am doing and not letting my mind wander. I concentrate fully on what I am doing. Secondly, the straightening of the knee. Every step I take, I straighten the knee. Even though I have had the odd fall, I'm not falling as often. I also find that I am walking much slower which allows me to concentrate with what I am doing. I will explain some of the falls I have had further on.

I will skip to January 2022. I was walking around the units just strolling along and I must admit I was in another world, not concentrating on what I was doing, and then all of a sudden, the left knee gives way. I know where I'm going but I cannot do anything about it. Down I went, landing on both knees and scraping them. I laid next to a parked car and using the car pulled myself up, and I hobbled home. It would have taken me at least 10 minutes to get up. I don't know how I did this, but the big toe on my right leg got into the action as well and that was also scraped. It felt like the toe was broken. One good thing about the surgery I go to in Hastings, if there is an emergency, they will fit you in straight away to see the nurses. I was able to go straight down and have the wounds attended to. They wanted to see me every second day to dress the wounds. It took over a month for them to heal.

The progress of the IBM is that it has now advanced to my arms. I have been having problems getting out of a chair for quite a while. I must be aware of what chair I sit in. If it is too low, I cannot get out without help. As you are aware, when you push yourself up from a chair, you use both hands to push yourself. Thus, the muscles in your arms get used. What happens if you got no muscles in your arms? Nothing to use, nothing to help push you up. You just can't do it.

In February 2022, I have to visit Kelly. Seeing the chairs in the surgery are too low, while waiting, I decide to stand up. She had an emergency and kept me waiting for over 40 minutes. When I was called, I hobbled down the hallway towards her rooms and lost my footing and arse over turkey I went. It is a wonder you did not hear the bang from where you were sitting. By golly, I fell hard. Both knees, toes, and an elbow copped it. This time for the first time, I grazed my forehead. Mate! They came from everywhere. Doctors, nurses, you name it. They are all there. Kelly said, "At least you picked the right place to fall." When you have a fall at my age, the whole body seems to ache. The nurses patched me up and attended to all wounds. Here we go again, back to the nurse's station every two days to have the wounds redressed. Came home, walked into the kitchen, did not lift my feet, and tripped over a mat and again, down I went. Where did I land? You are right, landed on the knees. OUCH. I had to crawl on my wounded knees to my lift chair in the lounge room; it was only about three metres. Try doing that with grazed knees. I was having the day from hell, two falls and a very bruised ego.

It was around the time of the day when I took the dog for a walk, grabbed my walker from the garage, took three steps outside, and the unbelievable happened. BOTH knees went; I went down like a tonne of bricks. If somebody was watching, they would have had a good laugh to see an old bastard like me fall the way I did. I thought the previous falls hurt; they were just trials. This was the real thing. Again, on to the knees. Boy, have they taken a beating today. This is the third time and the hardest fall today. Holding onto the walker does not help as I have not got the muscle strength in the arms to hold me up so when I'm ready to go down, I just go. I lay on the ground for a good 25 minutes, feeling sorry for myself. I tried to get up, but I couldn't. My arms could not lift me. There was no need for me to call Jeanette; she would have been unable to do anything to help, so I crawled into the garage onto some carpet, leaving a trail of blood behind. I had a huge challenge in front of me: how the bloody hell do I get up. My capacity to lift myself had diminished big time and as usual, there was no one around to help me and again, I did not have the alarm on me. Thought I would have learned that lesson by now. As usual, I learned the hard way. I found a towel to wipe away some of the blood from my knees. My tracky dacky's were stuffed. They had holes in both the knees. They probably helped to protect the knees a little when I fell.

The interesting part of my falls is the way I fall. It feels like I'm falling forward, but I don't. I tend to go straight down thus, the full weight of my body lands on my feet. The knees are forward, that's why I land on them. The feet also end up with grazes on the ankles and the toes. After many of my falls, I feel that I have broken the odd toe. They really ache. Nothing can be done for a broken toe, so it just has to take its own course.

The dilemma was still with me—how the hell do I get up. I noticed a large box which had two bar stools in it unopened. Maybe I could pull myself up onto that. I tried every way to hang onto it and lift myself up. With my hands also being the way they are, it is very hard to grip onto something when your fingers don't bend. I ended up giving the box a bear hug and eventually pulled myself onto the top. I was bloody exhausted. I sat there for at least 15 minutes. Finally hobbling inside, it was great to sit down, have a Coke, relax a little before calling the surgery, giving them the news of my latest fall. Back to the surgery, I went for a total review of my new wounds. Unfortunately, the dog missed out on his walk. The damage to the body was: both knees badly grazed. The graze is on the whole knee and not just a part of it. Big toe on the right leg grazed, ankle on the right leg also grazed. It took close to three months of continual care, having the dressings changed between two and four days apart before the wounds actually healed. The surgery is more than aware of the wounds becoming infected, so antibiotics were prescribed. The surgery certainly operates it in a different way than the way I used to. The old wives' way to heal a wound was to cover it, let it dry out, wait for a scab to form, then gradually pick the scab off. The new way is to treat the wound with an antiseptic cream, keep it covered, keep doing this, change the dressing every two days, keep it moist. Eventually, the wound will start to dry out on its own with a very little scab. I prefer the old way—you're not changing bandages every second day.

Since that drastic day, I have not had any significant falls outside. I now do remember to keep my knee straight, and I'm more than aware of the situation. I seem to hobble along. I also walk slower. I am reluctant to take large steps; it seems better and safer to take the smaller steps. My alarm is worn religiously when I'm outside.

In the last two months, I have had two falls both

inside. The first one, I got up from the table, turned around, walked near the toilet, and then fell. Both knees decided to give way. Why? I was not concentrating on my walking. I was thinking of what I wanted to do in the next room. The farthest thing from my mind was my walking. Again, as usual, everything landed on my right ankle, thus, I sustained a minor break. They did not plaster it as it was not serious enough. it healed in about a month. Thank God, that is my only break from a fall.

The next one is a doozy walking out of my bedroom with only my socks on my feet. One of the socks crept up about six inches and I tripped over it. I stumbled falling forward, hitting my head on the toilet door frame. While falling, I hit my hand on the toilet door, landed on my bony bum, as well as hurting my shoulder. The same scenario: how do I get up? I crawled into my bedroom where I had a box at the end of the bed and tried to climb up onto that. With my weak arms and quads, there is no hope in hell that I was going to get up onto the bed.

I remembered the contraption I had set up in the toilet with the hoist and sling. I had not taken it down, so let's see if this will work. It was all set up. All I had to do was press the button to bring the sling down, putting the sling under both arms. I asked Jeanette to hold me once I was lifted. Pressed the up button and up I went. It worked. What a bloody beauty, sitting there all this time and at last,

I have found a use for it. Getting up problem finally solved. The problem is solved while I am inside and near the toilet where it is set up. If I'm outside, it is a totally new scenario. We will have to come up with some ideas for the outside situation. It is fine if you have somebody strong around you. They can lift you up. If there is no one around, you are in trouble. So far, so good. Of the falls that I have had outside, I have been able to get up on my own. It has been a struggle but still on my own. I've yet to have a major problem outside. Let's hope it stays that way.

If you check with most medical suppliers, there is nothing portable available to lift someone up outside if they have a fall. The only options are to either ring an ambulance or find a couple of very strong people to help lift you up. This is not recommended as an easy way to do your back in is to lift someone especially with a dead weight.

This is where my idea of the hoist on an A-frame would certainly come in handy. Maybe this idea should be pushed. The problem would be where and who would keep them; you can't have one stuck on every street corner so to speak. Anyway, just a thought.

CHAPTER 10

It is now October 2022. It has been three and a half years since IBM was diagnosed. Let's have a look how my body has changed in this period. The weight has fallen off me at a slow rate. I now weigh around 75 kg. If you look at me in the mirror, I look like a prisoner of war. When the Holocaust survivors were discovered, they were skin and bones. That's how I look. Even my pot is starting to be affected. The arms and legs have no muscle on them at all, my forearms are also getting thinner, my face is also starting to lose tone. The fingers on both hands cannot bend; I cannot make a fist in either hand, yet my thumbs are not affected. Just looking at my hands you would think there is nothing wrong with them unless you see me try to use them.

Up until about six weeks ago, I did not suffer any pain from any of the muscle loss. My hands up until then were okay. Now, for some unknown reason, my hands just ache continuously. Also, from my shoulder down to my elbow, mate, the pain is unbelievable. I have thought maybe my hands are suffering from osteoarthritis or something similar. I have started to take glucosamine to hopefully ease the pain in my hands. So far, it has not worked. My GP is trying different pain relief, starting off with Para Osteo, a slow-release tablet taken up to four times a day. I think they're only good for low pain threshold. We then went onto Celecoxib up to three times a day; they are useless. The GP and I are talking once a week to try and get the right combination that takes the pain away; nothing works yet. Next cab off the rank was Endone, which is one of the number one pain killers. Bugger me, they did not work either. I said to Kelly I think we have three choices. Number one, you find something that will work; second, call an ambulance and they will take me to hospital and hopefully get to the bottom of where the pain is coming from; and third, refer me to a pain management specialist and hope they can come up with something. Kelly said, "Don't worry, Wayne. There are plenty of tablets that we have not tried. The next one will be the patch. It is called Buprenorphine, 5mg. As the name suggests, it has some morphine in it. You put the patch on your arm, and it lasts a week." So we tried it. Finally, at long last, some relief I find. It seems to work during the day. There is no pain at all, but first thing in the morning, starting around 3:00 a.m., the pain is unbearable. My arms feel like they are falling off. While I'm relaxed, that's when the pain occurs. It has got me stuffed. I have tried additional tablets at this time of the morning with no luck; nothing seems to work. The pain has started to come at night time, at around 8:30 p.m. for an hour or so. WHY? Again, there is no reason it should come and go the way it does. Kelly, at our last telephone conference, has increased the dose on the patch to 10 milligrams. Let's hope this works. I don't know if this has any bearing on the pain I'm getting, but I'm out of the OSTERINE. That's the concoction that my mate, Phil, makes. I have been out of it for about six weeks. I've asked Phil to make me another batch. We have often wondered if the product works. I've always said I do not want to stop it just in case it does or not. This, way we'll find out.

Kelly is concerned about my weight loss; five kilos just dropped off from nowhere. Something must be causing it. Let's try and find out what it is. We can't blame everything onto IBM, so she insisted that I have a colonoscopy. Alright for her, she has not got an arse that doesn't work. Once I take that muck, that makes you want to go to the loo. I will be in trouble. The IBM does affect the bottom hole. Normally if you need to go to the toilet, you just hang on and then go. In my case, if I want to go to the toilet, I can't hang on. I just go. It does not happen often but when I need to go, it just goes automatically. Many times, I've had an accident in my jocks because of this. The IBM has affected the muscles around my bottom hole. I do not seem to have the control to open and close when I want to. The muscles just don't want to work. They are so weak; I am unable to control it.

She has asked the hospital to keep me in overnight so that I do not have the problems at home like rushing to the toilet when it was necessary. They could control what was happening so that I did not have any accidents. I have been on the waiting list for close to three months. Hospitals are very busy now because of Covid, and there are no spare beds especially for a colonoscopy which needs special attention.

Had an appointment with the surgeon to check it all out. After an examination, he said there's no way that you have bowel cancer as you have not got any symptoms. What a relief! He asked me why I could not have a normal colonoscopy instead of going to hospital. I had to explain the reasons why; he certainly understood where I was coming from.

I'm quite happy; I don't want to have it done. I think we will just have to put up with the muscle tone getting lighter as the IBM progresses, which will inevitably make me lose weight.

Unfortunately, my gardening days are over. I cannot hold a shovel or pick anything large. I have not got the strength to push the shovel into the soil and turn it over. Even a fork to bust up the clogs is out of the question. The electric tools such as the hedge trimmer, large or small, I cannot again do. I just can't guide the instrument to where it should go. Also, the actual unit becomes too heavy anyway. Even small tools such as little forks and shovels, I find them difficult to hold. To pull a large weed out manually, again, I cannot do. I have not got the upper body strength to pull out a bloody weed—very disheartening. Last week, I was able to get a three-pronged hand tool and turn some soil over and pull-out small weeds. Hooray! I've finally able to make myself a little bit useful in the garden. I planted some tomatoes and cucumbers for the summer season. I will just have to try and maintain the little patch as best I can. We now have a gardener come in once every three months to do the main hedges and bushes.

    I have noticed the large difference in my walking. I no longer take large steps. Small steps seem to be the norm as I'm aware of my knee having to be straight. I walk very carefully thus, eliminating the chances of falling over. I walk the dog daily; that is when my walker gets used. I'm not prepared to take the chance on a long walk. I religiously get the falling necklace and the walker and off I go. Bending down can be a challenge; my legs are so weak that I must bend down so carefully. If I'm not hanging onto anything, it makes me feel so vulnerable. I do it in slow motion, again trying to eliminate any chance of falling. I don't know if I've said this before: falling is one thing, getting up is another. I must be so careful that if I fall, I must have something to hang onto to get up. Even that would make it difficult, but at least I can try.

Most of the time, if I bend, I look for something to hang onto with one hand, again trying to avoid any chance of falling. I have acquired a pickup tool, hold it in one hand, squeeze the trigger, and you can pick smaller items up from any position—very handy. If the item I must pick up is flat, I have no hope in hell of picking the thing up; this is where the pick-up tool comes in handy. Up until now, I'm still able to drive; I do have difficulty holding the steering wheel as my fingers are unable to wrap around the wheel. This is where my thumb comes in handy and does most of the holding. I purchased a little knob which bolts onto the steering wheel and eliminates the holding of the wheel. The knob fits into the palm of your hand and freely spins. You can steer the wheel that way. I do find that it puts pressure on your hand, causing it to become more painful. It may work for a person who has a disability and no pain in the hands. I have left it on the wheel just because it is there; you do not have to use it. My doctor wanted me to have a blood test. There was no one around to drive me so into the car I went with the dog. I will give you the rundown of exactly happened on this little outing.

Adjusted the cushions on the front seat and hopped in, bashed my knee on the steering wheel column as the cushions made the seat a little higher, made myself comfortable, put my left hand over to try and grab the seat belt. My fingers had trouble getting it in my hand. I eventually did and had to push the seat belt into its holder which I've found hard to do. Finally, I did it so we were ready to go. My hands were having difficulty gripping the wheel, but I made do with what I had, pulled up at the surgery, and tried to get out. I had my left hand holding on to the parcel tray and my right hand pushing against the driver's seat, trying to give me leverage to lift my bum off the seat. After much pushing, I was able to get up. The doctor also left me a script for some new tabs to try, had my blood test, and back to the car I went, having to repeat the getting in process again. At this stage, I said to the dog, "Bugger this. There has to be an easier way."

Drove to the chemist having to repeat the getting out process again, picked up the script, back to the car, repeated it all over again, went home. I said to the dog, "That is the last time I will drive the car unless it is in an emergency." Getting into the car is a nightmare. Getting out of the car is a nightmare. Driving the car is a nightmare. My inability to hold the wheel is one day going to cause an accident which I do not want to have; the trouble getting in and out is not worth it. From now on, I will get someone to do all that for me except if I have to personally go to the doctor's or whatever. I will get someone to drive me, so ladies and gentlemen, my driving days are over.

CHAPTER 11

I was reading about a chap in the USA named Jerry King. He publishes videos and DVDs about IBM; he has produced hundreds of episodes about the subject. In several of his shows, he mentions functional writing scale (IBM-FRS).

The IBM-FRS is a 10-point functional rating scale for patients with inclusion body myositis and is considered a reliable and valid measure of disease severity. Below are the contents in this scale that was modified from the ALS-FRS:

1. **Swallowing**

    * -4 Normal
    -3 Early eating problems, occasionally choking.
    -2 Dietary consistency changes
    -1 Frequent choking
    -0 Need tube feeding

2. **Handwriting with dominant hand prior to IBM onset**

    -4 Normal
    -3 slow or sloppy; all words are legible.

*-2 Not all words are legible
-1 Able to grip pen but unable to write.
-0 Unable to grip pen.

3. Cutting food and handling utensils

-4 Normal
-3 somewhat slow and clumsy, but no help needed.
*-2 Can cut most foods although clumsy and slow, some help needed
-1 Food must be cut by someone but can still feed slowly.
-0 Needs to be fed.

4. Fine motor tasks, opening doors, using keys, picking up small objects

-4 Independent
-3 Slow or clumsy in completing task.
*-2 Independent but requires modified techniques or assistive devices
-1 Frequently requires assistance from caregiver.
-0 Unable

5. Dressing

-4 Normal
-3 Independent but with increased effort or decreased efficiency.
* -2 Independent but requires assistive devices modified techniques e.g. shirts without buttons, Velcro straps
-1 Requires assistance from caregiver for some clothing items.
-0 Total independence

6. **Hygiene {bathing and toileting}**

   -4 Normal
   -3 Independent but with increased effort or decreased activity.
   -2 Independent but requires use of assistive devices (shower chair, raised toilet seat, etc.)
   -1 Requires occasional assistance from caregiver.
   -0 Completely dependent

7. **Turning in bed and adjusting covers**

   -4 Normal
   -3 Somewhat slow and clumsy but no help needed.
   * -2 Can turn alone or adjust sheets, but with great difficulty
   -1 Can initiate, but not turn or adjust sheets alone.
   -0 Unable to or requires total assistance.

8. **Sit to stand**

   -4 Independent (without use of arms)
   -3 Performs with substitute motions (leaning forward, rocking but without use of arms)
   * -2 Requires use of arms
   -1 Requires assistance from a device or person.
   -0 Unable to stand.

9. **Walking**

   -4 Normal
   * -3 Slow or mild unsteadiness
   -2 Intermittent use of an assistive device (walker, cane

foot orthosis)
-1 Dependent on assistive device
-0 Wheelchair dependent

10. Climbing stairs

-4 Normal
-3 Slow with hesitation or increased effort: uses handrail intermittently
-2 Dependent on handrail
-1 Dependent on handrail and additional support (cane or person)
* -0 Cannot climb stairs

The maximum score is 40, and the higher the score, the better the functional status of the patient. The IBM-FRS addresses swallowing, handwriting, cutting food, handling utensils, dressing, hygiene, turning in bed, adjusting covers, sit to stand, walking, and climbing stairs.

The IBM-FRS corelates well with isometric strength and manual muscle testing, and we believe it should be utilised as an end point measurement in future IBM trials. Also, to note, compared to other outcome measures, the IBM-FRS was also the most sensitive measure of change in a one study.

CHAPTER 12

The score relating to this test are as follows: between 34 and 40 equals stage one; between 16 and 33 equals stage 2; between 0 and 15 equals stage 3. The first time I did this test was on the 17th of November 2022. I will put an * on each of my score. I had a score of 21 which equals stage 2.

Let us run through each individual section and tell you how I came to that score.

1. Swallowing, score of 4 - Normal

I have found since IBM that I do have to chew my food a lot more than normal. If any of the pieces are too large, I have trouble swallowing. this has not changed much at all in the last three years.

2. Handwriting (with dominant hand prior to IBM on set), score of 2 - Not all words are legible

This is one area I have big trouble with. I used to pride myself on my handwriting. People commented on how nice a script I had. Over the three years, it is gradually getting worse. Once the fingers don't bend, you cannot hold the pen thus, your writing turns into scribble. If I write slow—very slow—I can print words. The other day, I had to sign some papers and I was barely able to write my name. I got by, but it was very difficult. Also, I can only use certain pens; ballpoints are a no-go. The only pen that I am able to use is one with a felt tip or a gel pen. The experts have come up with a rubber piece which you put on the part of the pen that your fingers grip, thus, making it easier to hold. In my case, I find that just as difficult so back to the drawing board. It is only a matter of time before I'm unable to write it all. If I must fill out a large number of forms, I now get my son, Shane, to act as my power of attorney, which he has been appointed legally.

3. Cutting food and handling utensils, score of 2 - Can cut most foods, although clumsy and slow; some help needed.

Seeing I am the chief cook and bottle washer, I have been in the kitchen ever since I retired. I was a cook in the Royal Australian Navy and have done heaps of cooking at home. For the last three years, it has become more difficult every day; it seems to get harder. I would like to devote more time to the subject as it does involve a lot of utensils. To give you one idea, try cutting an onion into diced pieces, say for spaghetti bolognese. It is very hard to hold the onion and very hard to hold the knife so both hands struggle. I will delve into this at a later stage.

4. Fine motor tasks (opening doors, using keys, picking up small objects), score of 2 - Independent but requires modified techniques or assistive devices.

This is definitely an area where I need help, not so much people's help but more on gadget help. The only doors that I can open are the ones with a handle, not an actual knob. I have fitted all doors with knobs. A little silicon device, they are called doorknob grips which fit onto the actual knob, thus, when you grab it, you grab the silicon or the rubber which makes it easy to grip and turn the knob for you. I purchased several of these from Amazon. The only problem with them is they are very flimsy and do not seem to last long if they get a lot of use. I have already purchased a second lot as a couple have not lasted the distance; they work out at around $25 a pair.

Using keys? Ha! That does happen only if the key is on a key ring. Grabbing an individual key? I just cannot hold it; the muscle tone in the fingers makes it difficult to join the finger and thumb together to hold the key. If the keys are on the key ring, I can hold the key ring even though I still have trouble. I'm able to do it on some keyholes, not all. I do have trouble with the front door. What I find I do most times is I leave the bloody door unlocked, eliminating the key problem. Only yesterday, I came home with two keys on a ring. I opened the door beautifully. Do you think I could get the bloody key out of the hole? I pushed, I pulled, I turned as best I could but to no avail. How frustrating is this. I just could not get a grip on the key. I'm so glad I have calmed down and don't do my block as easily as I used to. Otherwise, the key would have been thrown in the bin as well as the bloody lock. It took me 10 minutes to get the key out of the lock. From now on, I will leave the bloody door unlocked. Lesson learnt.

Picking up small objects is a task. I was given a gadget with a handle on it. It is called a pickup device. Press the trigger, the tongs join at the end, making it easy to pick small items up. It does not work for bigger items as the tongs are not strong enough as well. I can't lift heavy items anyway. If I must pick up a small item off the floor, I bend over very gingerly. When I bend, the legs get wobbly. If I'm not careful, arse over I go. I have found the more careful I try to be, the clumsier I become. The number of times I have put things in the rubbish bin and missed the bloody hole, spilling whatever I was ready to put in, then having to bend over or get my little gadget to pick it up. Every morning, I have to get our tablets ready. That's all good unless I drop some, then the games begin. I just cannot pick up an individual tablet no matter how big or small it is. I have to push it off the table so that I can put it into the palm of my hand; this enables me to put it where it has to go.

5. Dressing, score of 2 - Independent but requires assistive devices or modified techniques (Velcro strips, shirts without buttons, etc.)

Dressing has been a major problem since this all started. Anything with buttons on it forget it. I cannot do a button up for the life of me. I cannot grab the zipper only, If the zip has an extension or even a paper clip on it, then I can pull it up or down. Whenever clothing is purchased, I'm limited to what I can wear so trousers must have an elastic waist. Most trousers do not have that option, which means I can get away with wearing tracksuit pants. Shirts with buttons are a no; only polo or t-shirts with no buttons are suitable. I used to always wear jeans and would purchase up to 10 pairs at a time, meaning I would get them cheaper. I have not been able to wear jeans for a couple of years; no jeans have the elastic waist and all have zips at the front, so the last lot I purchased were donated to the Salvation Army. They will certainly get the use out of them. Unfortunately, I just could not wear them.

I find the hardest thing to get into are socks. I can put the sock on the left foot very easily. There is no way that I can get it onto my right foot. I have to guide the end over my toes. I then had to get a pair of pliers and pull the rest over my foot. The pliers I have are curved at the end which makes them a lot easier to use. With my forefinger and thumb on either hands not touching, it makes it very hard to grab hold of anything, let alone clothing. It is almost impossible to pull your underpants and pants up after you go to the toilet as well as while you are dressing. I tuck my hand into my trousers and use the back of the hand to adjust and pull up at the same time. It does seem strange that you must lie down and wriggle from side to side to put your pants on. One annoying thing I find is when your underpants start to slip down and you cannot grab them to pull them up. I now make sure there is plenty of elastic in any jocks that I wear. Same with trousers, the elastic must be very firm. Lifting your arms above your head to put a shirt on can be challenging. While I have the pain in my arms, it is difficult but as usual, we get by. We find a way. Can't let little things like this get in my way.

Most of my old clothes have been thrown out or donated. I have kept one good going-out shirt. My shirts consist of polo and t-shirts. My trousers are new, and all have elastic waists. My jocks are kept relatively new as long as the elastic is fine. All of my socks are made of thin cotton as the thicker ones are too hard to put on. All of my shoes are what is called no tie. On the last hole on both sides where the laces go, two knobs with a hook on each lace are put in place. The laces tie around one knob then the hook fits into the other knob, eliminating the need to do them up great idea.

6. Hygiene (bathing and toileting), score of 2 - Independent that requires use of assistive devices (Share a chair, raised toilet seat, etc.)

In the shower, I do have a chair I no longer use as I cannot get out of it. It just sits there and holds the shampoo and other things. I no longer use bars of soap. I cannot hold them. I now use liquid soap in a pump bottle and a flannel or face washer. The flannel is getting harder to hold and reach under my arms. and my feet I dare not bend; even less room in the shower than there is outside of it. Washing my face is getting harder; I have difficulty lifting my arms above my head, let alone holding onto a face washer at the same time. I put a little soap on my hand, reach up to my ears, and give them a good scrub. My right hand is worse than my left; my left hand must do both ears.

Drying is now starting to become a challenge. I can just hold the large beach towel but it's getting far too heavy; the ordinary bath towel is also becoming too heavy, so I'm looking for a lighter one that I can use. To dry my back, I must lay the towel on the bed, lay myself on it, and move around until the back is dry. All the towels in our collection are becoming too heavy to even lift. I don't think I'm very far away from personal help. I will plod along on my own if I can. Toileting has been discussed previously; all I can say is that without the bidet, I would be totally stuffed. It washes and dries the most delicate parts.

7. Turning in bed and adjusting covers, score of 2 - Can turn alone or adjust sheets, but with great difficulty

You don't realise that the IBM takes its toll in so many ways. You roll over in bed and the covers fall off you. You then try to lift the covers with your arm and hand and find that you are unable to do so. The covers for my arms are too heavy. So, what I try and do is to have my knees and legs under the covers and lift the leg, which then helps lift the covers. Certainly, not rocket science. I have yet to come up with any ideas as to how to make this problem easier for me. Maybe, a lighter linen.

It is harder in the winter as you have heavier bed clothes. We are now entering Australian summer so the bed clothes will be lighter. I've only had this problem in the winter. At this stage, let's hope the summer will be a lot easier to handle.

8. Sit to stand, score of 2 - Requires use of arms

Probably one of the most challenging of situations that we have. Anywhere you go, there are chairs; the amount of chairs that do not have armrests is amazing. You will find that in most places you go, all the chairs are plain old chairs. Naturally catering for the norm, but as you go through life, you learn everything is not the norm. There are people who have special needs and chairs with armrests is one of them. As you grow older, it is much harder to get out of a chair without an armrest. Like the oldies, you have people like me who have a medical condition. The surgery which I visit have changed all of the chairs to ones with armrests. I don't think it was only me who was having a problem getting out of them. Whenever I go to the surgery, I take my walker with me and use that to sit on while I'm waiting. I find it easier to get out of that than any of their chairs even with armrests. With IBM, you unfortunately lose the ability to be able to rise out of a chair without the help of your arms and as I am finding now, my arms are not much use anyway. So whenever I sit, it does not matter where it is. I study the chair to make sure I can get out of it. If it is too low, there is no hope of getting out. Nowadays, Shane comes with me to most of my appointments, and he lifts me out of any chairs I sit in.

In our lounge room, we now have four reclining chairs. Two of them are special lift chairs—one for the wife, one for me. The other two are mainly used by the dog and cat and of course, any visitors if they're game enough to get the dog or cat off first. If I sit on either recliner, I cannot get off, so I religiously use my lift chair. Each lift chair lifts you up so that you're near to a standing position. If I'm in a position where I can't get up, I have to rock backwards and forwards until I get enough momentum up to be able to stand—easier said than done. When somebody tries to help you get out of a chair, what they find difficult is that I am just a dead weight. I cannot help in any way, so they had to lift my whole-body weight at one time. Majority of people do struggle with this task; even I get frustrated. When a person is trying to help, it makes you feel so helpless and useless—very degrading.

I purchased an article from the USA. It is called a springer seat. What you do is set the seat to your weight. You then sit on it and when you are ready to get up, as soon as it detects a slight upward movement, the seat springs up, lifting you naturally. It cannot be used in a lot of areas. It is a little cumbersome—big enough for your bum to sit on but too big to put in the front seat of a car. So its uses are limited. I'm losing weight and each time I have to sit on it, I have had to readjust the settings to lesser weight. That, in itself, is a pain in the bum—having to reset it each time you want to use it. It is sitting in the bathtub now as I cannot find anywhere to use it. It turns out it was a waste of money I think it was around $60. It's like the old saying, "Suck it and see." It was worth the exercise to find out what this thing could do.

I am also finding it very hard to get out of the car. I have put cushions and a swivel cushion on the driver's seat to give me a little bit of extra height. I then must hang on to the door with one hand and the seat with the other and try and push myself up. I'm finding it harder every time I have to get out. If I'm a passenger, the driver must come around and physically help me out. I'm having trouble with all sedans; any SUV which is taller I seem to be able to get out of those without help.

My driving days are limited so it does not pay for me to go out and buy an SUV.

9. Walking, score of 3 - Intermittent use of an assistive device (cane, walker])

Naturally, this is the area which finds you out all the time. Standing on your feet is the challenge. Walking without falling is the biggest challenge. We have discussed in a previous chapter about the straightening of the knee. Since I have been doing that, my walking has improved. I can now walk further distances if I need to. I tested myself out several months ago. I drove down to Red Rooster and the car would not start. I did not have my phone on me and the dick heads in the store were way too busy to let me use the phone, so I had to walk. I also had the dog with me who is suffering from cruciate ligament damage so with him on the leash, I made my way home. The distance is approximately three kilometres; the dog and I made it unscathed. It would have taken me at least an hour and a half but on the way, I did not stumble once and only stopped once to have a break. I was so proud of myself to walk that distance without any mishaps. I boasted to friends for weeks about it. I was able to ring roadside assist to have the car started. I did not walk back. One of my friendly neighbours gave me lift. That was quite an achievement by me.

I do find myself walking much slower and being aware of my knee straightening, I do sometimes stumble and have had near falls. Thankfully, I have escaped any mishaps. I do religiously wear my falling necklace when I walk any distance. If I do fall, at least the necklace will contact the people on the list. Also, my walker gives me more confidence and eliminates, or I should say lessens, the chance of a fall.

10. Climbing stairs, score of 0 - Cannot climb stairs.

In the early days of this disease, I did notice my inability to tackle rungs on a ladder. I will put my foot on the first step and found I was unable to lift my other foot to the second step. The muscles in my thighs were deteriorating at a rapid rate, and I just did not have the strength to lift my leg. We went on a cruise to New Zealand. One of the excursions was on a tour bus. I could not work out why I was having trouble getting up the first step. I had to ask help from the driver.

We were booked on several excursions, had to cancel

them because of my inability to get up the steps so any tours which would involve steps had to be cancelled. The only way I could negotiate stairs was to pull myself up by the rail. That was good fun getting up, but it was more fun trying to get down. You then had the added fear that you could fall; the easiest way was I was not to go up or down stairs or ladders at all.

CHAPTER 13

As I have mentioned before, I am the chief cook and bottle washer. Since I retired which has now been eight years, I have taken over in the kitchen. This has given Jeanette a big break from having to do the cooking. The kitchen is where your hands get used all the time and it is amazing and how we take it for granted—how the hands work. When they don't work, you need to get little gadgets to help you. In this chapter, we will discuss the gadgets that I use.

1. Can opener

I found that the normal can opener requires you to turn the handle. I cannot do it. I can put my fingers on the handle but do not have the strength to turn it. I purchased a battery-operated device which you place on top of the can, and it goes around, cutting the can on the side. For the opener to cut properly, it had to go around at least two times, sometimes three. This turned out to be a very slow process and annoying.

I could find myself doing my block with this device so I ordered an electric can opener where you place the can on the cutting section, and it does it automatically much better. Bo, the dog, is on a special kidney diet where I must open at least one can a day; this makes the task much easier.

2. Jar opener

Do you notice how many jars you open in the kitchen? this is an area which you just take for granted. I did not realise how often jars needed to be opened. I would normally get a large knife, hitting the side of the lid which loosened it. Now, I cannot even hold the knife, let alone having the strength to hit the side of the lid. There are so many different devices on the market. I think I've tried several of them, eventually finding one that works. Most of them require you to hold the jar in one hand and the device in the other. When both hands don't work, you find it difficult to do either. The one that I have chosen and works beautifully is the battery-operated opener. You place it on the jar and press the button. It has two sets of two little arms—one which holds the jar lid on two sides then one which holds the jar on two sides. When the jar is being held firmly, the other set of arms holding the lid turn it and open it. I have found that this unit will open most size jars, and you don't have to use your hands to hold it.

3. Bottle opener screw top

This is an area which covers soft drink bottles. This little device is made of metal two pieces joined in the middle with serrated sides. You open it up, place it over the top with one hand, and you pull the two sides together. You then turn it which turns the top. For the larger tops such as fruit juice and vinegar two litre bottles, you must use a different procedure. Maybe I could use the jar opener on this size bottle. I must try it later. I have a piece of rubber, 10 inches by 10 inches, very thin and sticky on both sides. It is like a towel. I do not know what it is called; it was given to me by one of our OTs. I'm still able to do this but for how much longer I don't know. I place the rubber over the lid and turn with my hand, loosening it. I then get a large knife, piercing the little pieces of plastic holding the lid on. You have to lay the bottle on its side to do this. You must be careful not to spill any of the contents. I have a couple of other gadgets that are very hard to use because both hands are needed.

4. Ring pull cans and lids

Two separate areas on this one. I cannot open a can of Coke with my fingers. I find it hard to lift the ring pull, believe it or not. I have not got the strength in my fingers to lift it. I'm able to get a knife, place it under the ring, and lift it up. I am able to do that at this stage. The ring pull lid is a different process again, or get a knife to lift the ring, then I get this little gadget shaped like a question mark made of plastic with a hook on one end. I place that hook on the ring, resting the circular part on the lid, then pull, and the lid comes off.

5. Tilting kettle

I cannot hold a kettle to pour water for tea or coffee. For a price of $160, we purchased a tilting kettle. The kettle is placed on a stand which has hinges on either side thus, enabling the kettle to be moved forward, tipping it up, and enabling it to fill the cups sitting in front of it. The user does not have to lift the kettle. You can you fill it by placing it under the tap. If you cannot do it that way, we get a cup, fill it with water, and transfer it to the kettle.

6. Eating Utensils

Knife, fork, and spoon I have huge difficulty in holding any of these utensils. I purchased modified versions of the above; all of these have been fitted with a larger padded handle which is made of rubber. It enables the user to hold them in your hand easier. The thickness of the handle moulds into your hand. The further along I travel with this journey, I am finding them more difficult to use each day. When you are trying to cut meat holding it with your fork and then trying to cut with the knife, it becomes very frustrating when the meat flies off the plate and lands in your lap. I no longer go out to a restaurant or a pub to have a meal; people are very cruel and stare at any person with a disability. As far as I am concerned, they won't be staring at me. It is hard enough doing it in front of your family, let alone strangers.

7. General gadgets

I have tried several other bits and pieces which is supposed to help you cut onions and tomatoes, but I find them useless. They are either sitting at the bottom of the drawer or have already been thrown out. Not worth talking about. I have not come across anymore actual products which help me in the kitchen. The ones I have listed are the main ones.

Let me talk about the problems I have in the kitchen. All our plates were in cupboards above my shoulder. They have now been moved to a lower position where I do not have to lift them above my shoulders. I am now finding it hard to lift the plates from the sink into the drying tray. The same applies to all our medicinal needs; they have also been moved to a lower position. All products in the pantry that get used all the time are at arm's reach.

I have two problems: I cannot reach too high, and I cannot bend too low. Unfortunately, not everything can be put in the centre to make life a lot easier. Once I get to the chopping board all sorts of problems arise. Peeling an onion is okay, chopping an onion not good. I can only hold the onion with one or two fingers. Also, holding the large kitchen knife presents problems. I cannot wrap my hand around the handle. I have to hold it with my thumb and a couple of fingers. We are able to get by but I don't know for how long. Chopping into smaller pieces is a lot harder. I find that they now sell chopped onions at the supermarket, but the pieces are a little large for some dishes. It is all trial and error.

Last week, I decided to make a coleslaw. Boy was this fun to cut the cabbage and I like it thin. It took me over half an hour to cut half of a cabbage. The three onions only had to be sliced; that only took me five minutes. I'm just glad that I did not have to grate the carrots; that was done with the electric grater All in all, from start to finish, it took me near an hour, normally 15 minutes.

Many people offer help in the kitchen. I tell them that while I can do it, let me do it as there will be a time soon when I will not be able to do a thing.

My long-nose bent pliers are a godsend. Without them, I would certainly have to find something else to use. As mentioned, they pull up my socks. They are used in the kitchen to open up the range hood, in the fridge to pull out draws, in the laundry to help me pull the soap holder out in the washing machine. Anything that I cannot grip that is when they come into use. Maybe I should have used them the other day with the front door key. Probably next time.

One area I am having big problems with is holding onto things. I find that I am dropping virtually everything that I pick up; it does not matter what shape it is. I just can't hold onto it. Lately in the kitchen, I have dropped a large kitchen knife several times, just missing my toes. Better be careful or I WILL be missing some toes. I will have to start doing what I do with my knees and that is to concentrate more on what I am doing as I do it. I can only carry one plate at a time, I cannot hold two, They're too heavy.

I find that we are now eating more of the frozen TV dinners. I have tried Lite N' Easy and Youfoodz. I find both of those very bland. I seem to prefer the ones you buy from the supermarket. At least it keeps me out of the kitchen for a little while.

We will list here in simple terms the things I can't do. I cannot do the following: tie up shoe laces , put shoes on without a shoe horn, pull my pants up, put on socks, hold a towel, dry myself after a shower, lift my leg to dry between my toes, hold a toothbrush to brush my teeth (I now use a battery-operated toothbrush), wash myself all over in the shower (I certainly miss some parts), lifting hands and arms above the head is difficult, opening bottles, opening cans, lifting a small bottle of beer and tipping it into a glass (I cannot hold the bottle), lifting either arm up with a fork or spoon to feed myself, picking up a cup or any bottle with one hand, lifting and putting it to my mouth to have a drink.

Hold a knife and fork and spoon to feed myself, cutting food on a plate, hold a kitchen knife (often when I go to pick the knife up, I drop it), prepare most food, hold a pen and write properly, type on a keyboard, stand from a seated position on any low chair, get up from the toilet, wipe my bum, fold paper, make a bed, most house work, most gardening, drive the car, climbing stairs, climbing a ladder, using nail clippers on fingers or toes, squeezing a pimple (I do not have the strength in my fingers to squeeze it), putting a pillow slip onto a pillow (tried that last week; honestly, it took me over 10 minutes to try and do it without any success; certainly not worth the hassle).

To have a cup of coffee is starting to be a problem. I am unable to pick a cup or a can with one hand so I must pick up receptacle with two hands, have my elbows on the table, and guide both hands to my mouth. Just lifting my hands to my mouth with nothing in them or even to scratch my nose is number one painful, as well as being very difficult to do. I'm now starting to use a straw more often with hot and cold drinks. I now notice that when lying in bed, if I lay the arm stretched out to my side, I am unable to lift the arm up to bring it back down to my side. I must use my left arm to reach over and guide the right arm to its side. The left arm is not affected. Also, while sitting at the kitchen bench, I find it difficult to lift my right arm up to my face many times. I have to use my left hand to guide the right arm to wherever I want it to go. Again, the left arm is not affected. I could list many more things I cannot do. To summarise, just work out what you use your hands and arms for, and I'm affected in some way with everything you use them for.

The area I have the most fun with is eating peanuts or potato chips or small snacks, I just cannot pick them up between my finger and thumb or any finger and thumb; it certainly is a challenge.

Also, my forearms are now starting to hurt against the marble bench; it is starting to be bone on bench, no padding in between. I'm using a folded towel to rest my arms on. Every day, I use this; it does help to eliminate the pain, which only occurs when I don't use the towel.

I will stop it there as you can see; I could go on and on. I wish someone would jam this fucking disease to where the sun doesn't shine.

I am certainly having some difficulty getting out of my bed. Usually, you push yourself up with both arms and then out you get, I'm now unable to push myself up therefore, I roll around onto my back then creep forward on my bum till I get to the edge of the bed. I then move to and fro forward, giving me the momentum to stand up. I decided to invest in a hospital bed, hoping that the lifting device would make my life easier. I contacted Renee, our case manager, to see if we had the funds to purchase it through our package and not our own pockets. She said we did have the funds, and we did qualify for such a purchase.

The stupid part is that we cannot purchase this product or any product unless our OT has recommended that we need it. If there is no mention in any assessment he has made of the product we're talking about, it cannot be purchased. He charges around about $300 for a visit and an assessment; we had to go through all this bullshit before we could start looking. The OT also must be there to look at the bed and recommend which one we should purchase. The company who sells the beds must clarify that all this has been done. Otherwise, they cannot sell bed to us.

We met at a disability shop situated in Mornington where they had three beds on display. The OT explained to us the ups and downs and the ins and outs of each bed; they were all single beds and included a king single and a long single and an ordinary single. We chose the king single with a special set of satin sheets. The satin was in the middle of the sheet, which made it easier to move your legs if you had problems with your legs which I do. Also, the mattresses come in different thicknesses so we had to get one which was very comfortable while we were at it. The mattress on the beds in the hospitals is of basic thickness and as we know not very comfortable at all.

One thing they agreed to do, which was very important was, to remove the queen-sized mattress and base that we already had at home. At normal rates, the cost of removal is normally $150. That turned out to be a good saving.

After a very good look around and a good demonstration by the shop assistant, we settled on a king single. The price, includes the delivery by two people as the bloody thing weighs a tonne and also pick up and disposal of the other mattress and base. I must not forget the satin sheets which turned out to be $90 each. I nearly fainted at that price—all up $4,500. There is no way known that if I had to pay for this bed myself that I would spend that much. Here's me having a go at other people routing the system, and I am doing exactly the same thing (not really). I don't set the prices; the company who sells the product in the first place are the ones who are doing that to the system.

Two young guys, around early 20s and plenty of muscles, delivered the new bed. I asked if they could do us a favour before they moved the new bed into the front room; and that was remove Jeanette's old bed outside and move my bed into the front room. to replace her bed. This made my room free for the new bed. Nothing phased these guys; they were very happy to do anything we wanted. Just the night before, Jeanette had a little accident on her mattress, and there was a stain present. Best to throw that one out and keep the good one. The new bed was bought in along with the new mattress, and they set it up. Before leaving, they gave us a full demonstration on how to use the same. They loaded the old mattress onto the truck and away they went. My main concern is getting used to a single bed; the last time we slept in one would have been when I was single. That would have had to be a minimum of 54 years ago.

Since I have had the bed, I still find it hard to get out. It is too much mucking around, lifting the head end up, getting you into the seating position, so I still roll around on to my back, doing the same as before. My biggest problem is my arms don't work; we just must do the best we can with what we've got. One very good point about the bed is that it does go down close to ground level. The height of the bed and the mattress is probably about 12 inches. I went to ground the other day to test it, knowing that I cannot get up normally. So I went to the bed and was able to put myself onto the mattress, then use the control to lift myself up that way. It is a much easier way to get up on to my feet than using my hoist, which I have only used a couple of times anyway. As the OT would say, a lot safer—no chance of any mishaps while in use.

One area I mentioned is getting out of bed. I have found that the bed has been facing the wrong way. When I get out, I move my body to the right then wiggle my way round so that I can stand up. I have since moved the bed so to get out of it, I'll move my body to the left; this makes it a lot easier to stand, and I don't have to wriggle as much. That problem was easily solved.

Unless you are involved with a person who has IBM, the average person would not know what the disease is. Naturally, the same applies to friends. They just do not understand what you are going through, or they don't really care; it's one or the other. One of our best friends is forever inviting us to their house. At the front of the house are the front stairs, at least 20 of them. I keep telling him that it is an impossibility for me to get up the bloody things; they were not happy until we accepted an invite.

He kept saying, "All will be fine. You'll get up these stairs easily." The day of reckoning finally came. I had a look at the stairs in front of me. Oh my God, there is no way humanly known that I will climb the stairs. He said, "I will give you a hand." After two rungs, he gave up and so did I. I said to him, "Mate, I told you that I would not get up the stairs but you kept insisting. The only way to convince you that I could not do it was to show you. Now you know." It goes to show that most people don't listen to what you say in the conversation; they will just nod and agree with what you say, not really taking in what you are talking about. One thing I do not do is advertise the fact that I have IBM; people don't ask, and I don't volunteer the information. I did explain to these friends what my condition was and what I can do and can't do. It actually took a demonstration to prove my point.

Our house is not a difficult place to get around with IBM. The front and back entrance have had ramps put in which eliminates the steps. Special handrails have also been fitted to hang onto if needed. Two lift chairs have replaced the couch. There are barstools at the bench. The toilet has a special seat, all enabling the user to get out of the chairs without any fuss.

When you go to a friend's house or any other house, none of these changes have been made. The easiest way to avoid these problems is to not go out in the first place. Even today, I come across a situation. My friend next door and myself take my dog for a walk on a daily basis. I rang her to see if everything was fine. She said, "Come and meet me at my house. I have someone I'd like you to meet." So off I went to meet her, I have explained that when I walk, I have my alarm and also my walker with me. When I arrived, she said, "Leave your walker here. I would like you to meet a friend." This is in their backyard; to meet her friend I would have to have negotiated a large step. I said, "Sorry guys, there is no way known I can get up that step." She said, "What do you mean? It's only small." I replied, "It may be small to you, it's bloody big to me." She then said, "I will help you." Again, I said, "Let's give it a miss. I will not be able to do it even with your help." The husband interrupted and said, "Come on, what's the matter with you? You should be able to get up that small step." I then said, "Sorry, guys, I know what I am capable of and I will not be able to negotiate your step." She suggested that I use the house step to come in. I had a quick look and said no to that one as well; I know what my capabilities are.

I then she said to her, "I have no steps in my house. I have eliminated them all by putting ramps in. You must understand my position. I know I come across as unsociable but it is not that at all, and until people understand what IBM is and what it stops you from doing, you will then realise why I do not visit people. It is because of this situation." And it is also embarrassing for me not being able to please people. Once again, I apologised. I think to myself these people know or I have explained to them what IBM is. and what it does to my body. They have known for a long time that I cannot climb a step, yet they still invite you in, expecting you to have performed a miracle on yourself and have recovered or may be able to do these things. I could feel their annoyance at me being unable to do what they wanted me to do. Hey, guys, I'm not going try to do something that I know I cannot do just to make you happy; the only one that has to be happy is me.

CHAPTER 14

So far, the whole story line has been about me. I think it only fair that I share with you what my partner of 54 years is sharing with me. We're both in this together and always have each other's back.

As mentioned earlier, she was diagnosed with frontal lobal dementia in 2019 and short-term memory loss. I won't delve into the disease as I've already done it. She is 75 years of age, born in 1947, and for a lady at that ripe old age, the only tablet she takes is to prevent a urinary tract infection from happening. She has had UTI before and it has played heavily on her, being admitted to the hospital on two occasions. The first occasion was after the weekend from hell. She went to Rosebud Hospital where she stayed for approximately one week; they treated her for UTI for that period then let her home. The second time, the ambulance people took her to Frankston and again treated her for UTI; she also stayed for a week and then they let her out. The hospital not once mentioned how to avoid UTI, so we left it up to the GP to prescribe the appropriate tablets.

She's probably a little overweight but at her age, who cares? Doctors are certainly surprised that she is on no other medications.

The only major problem was a left hip replacement in 2014; other than that, the body has stood up well. She now finds she cannot get moving around the house without the aid of a walker; this enables her to get around okay. During a visit to the doctors or anywhere else she must go, you will also see her use the walker.

I had mentioned earlier about her weekend from hell. Well, once she goes to ground, you can't get her up. If I go to ground, I can crawl to wherever I have to with great difficulty to lift myself up. Unfortunately, Jeanette cannot do that. She weighs around 100 kg and finds it hard to crawl anywhere, so she is stuck wherever she lands. I have often wondered if the dementia is causing this—where the brain is not telling the body what to do, or is it just plain laziness where she can't be bothered putting her body through a little pain naturally to get some gain. She does not do any type of exercise, other than the odd walk with me or one of the carers to take the dog for a walk. Maybe we should get a physio in and get her to do some exercises which may make her more mobile. She must be always encouraged to get her to do anything on her own unless there is somebody there to push her along; there's no way known that whatever you want her to do will she do it on her own.

Regarding her going to ground, we have been unable to come up with any solution other than call an ambulance or ask Shane to do it. I have looked high and low on the internet, eBay and several disability stores for some different gadgets to use, but you need more than one person to do it. With my muscle tone, I cannot do it on my own. I have noticed on some disability sites where you can buy a machine which runs along the ceiling, the length of the house, or one room; it moves along on rails. You position the device where the person is lying and you lower the sling and you lift her/him up and then move them to where they have to go. I think the cost would be prohibitive. It runs into the thousands; if money was no object, you would probably do it.

Also available on the market is what they call a lifting machine. This type of machine is battery-operated which can lift a person into a standing position or in and out of bed, or even into a chair. The big problem is, it is large and cumbersome—very hard to handle. A minimum of two persons is required to use the unit. Naturally, safety is the number one priority. The machine on its own is worth up to $3,000.

She's probably very lucky in one way that she does not comprehend what is going on with me; she keeps forgetting. It does not affect her in any way. Is that a good thing? I personally think it's one less problem she or I must deal with. Me being her carer, the less the better.

We do find that the dementia is getting worse; all seems the same with everyday doings but every now and then, something comes up which raises red flags. The last couple of weeks we have found that she is unable to get out of bed on her own. She lies sideways and finds that her arms are unable to push her up just like me, but she has not got IBM. The brain is not telling the body what to do. We have had to change the time the carers come here; we have changed it all to mornings so they can lift her out of bed and shower her. This has been working fine for three days a week; they also help her to get dressed. We find showering once every two to three days is acceptable. She does not do any strenuous work or anything that would raise a sweat. She does wear incontinence pads so washing that area daily is a necessity. All the carers seem to pat it down and know exactly what to do and when to do it; that eases the burden on me. That is the very reason that we have them come in.

Two weeks ago, on Monday morning, she had problems getting up. When the carer and I finally got her up and dressed, she had difficulty walking and was disorientated, not really knowing where she was and where she was going. It seemed that she was in another world. I did not muck around. I said to the carer I will call an ambulance. She's having difficulty doing everything. I thought it might have been the UTI; all signs were familiar to previous times when she had it. The ambulance arrived and after at least 30 minutes, the paramedics were ready to take her to hospital. To Rosebud Hospital she went. The doctors kept her in for over a week. They ruled out UTI and were more concerned that the dementia was getting worse. The doctors and social workers liaised together; they would not let her out if she was to come home. If I was the only person there, they felt that with my IBM, I would be unable to care for her suitably. They insisted that she be sent to respite for a minimum of two weeks. Just recently learned how all this works. The government allows a person 63 days per year that they can use for RESPITE. What this does is it gives a person the opportunity to settle in with the home we have chosen. The respite can be used in blocks of 14 days. You are unable to take the person out of the care for more than one day; the only way it can be done is if the care is terminated. Take the time away and hope that a bed be available in the same home if you want to go back. My hands are being tied by all the red tape. What I want to do is take her out for a week, see if she can handle it or not. If she can handle it, she stays at home. If she can't handle it, then she goes back to respite which would then eventually lead to permanent care. But they will not allow me to take that week. Bloody bureaucrats. While the person is in RESPITE, her My Aged Care allowance and her package continues to be funded, but while she's in respite, the package stays on hold, and you cannot use it—a little bit of double dutch there. The reason why they only allow two weeks at a time is if you want, you can try another nursing home if you are not quite happy with what is happening with the one you are at. You do hear many stories about what nursing homes should do and shouldn't do. There are many nursing homes that do not have beds available for RESPITE. They only handle permanent patients. the number of homes we contacted was mind-boggling; I just could not believe the amount that do not have respite patients.

We have found a nursing home in the next suburb up from us. They do care for RESPITE patients. We have booked her in for the minimum amount of time which is two weeks. It is up to her if she improves in the next two weeks, she can come home. If she doesn't improve, we will have to extend the RESPITE for another two weeks then unfortunately, we will have to look at extending the respite for a longer period. In total, we can have 63 days overall. We will then have to look at permanent care. It is all play-it-by-ear game at this stage.

They have placed her in the high-dependency dementia section; there would be at least 20 rooms on this floor. I do not think that all the rooms are taken as there only seems to be at least six other persons in the ward. Each patient is able to move and walk wherever they want without supervision.

I do have a nickname for this section. I call it the zombie ward; most times the patients are sitting there, sky gazing, staring into space all without supervision. The more I see this place, the more I want Jeanette out of the joint. I do not want her to join the zombie brigade. I have seen the nurses or carers interacting with the patients but not very often. I suppose there is a limit of what you can do with each person. I'm sure Jeanette would say if she knew what was going on, "For Christ's sake, get me out of this fucking place." Anyway, she does not have to say it because I am saying it.

She herself seems to have accepted the nursing home very well, has not complained about coming home, and seems to have fitted in quite well. The objective in the short term is we have to get her as close to normal as we can. The question is: can the dementia be kept at bay? I saw her every day this week. This is a daily rundown of what happened:

DAY ONE - All good. Very happy and comfortable, stayed in her room, was unable to get out of any chair or the toilet without help.

DAY TWO – All good. Very happy and comfortable, stayed in her room unable to get out of any chair or the toilet without help.

DAY THREE - All very good. Comfortable. Was out of the room mixing with other patients, was able to get out of the chair and the toilet by herself without any help at all—a large improvement.

DAY FOUR - Poor day. Stayed in bed all day. Did not look well. I missed the next day but went in the day after.

DAY FIVE - This day was the best we could have hoped for. She was in excellent spirit. Was able to get out of the chair, also off the toilet. Everything looked hunky dory, that is what we need. If she can show that for four days in a row, she can come home.

DAY SIX - Another day where she was out mixing with other residents. When I arrived, the nurse was throwing a balloon to the residents, and they were hitting it back. They had Christmas carols playing in the background. Jeanette was really into this, singing along and playing with the balloon. Could not have cared less if I was there or not. The nurse tried to move her from the chair; there was no way that she could have gotten out of that chair as it was too low. She would not let any of the nurses touch her. She fought them all the way. I decided to go home, let them sort it out. Bad day for our future outcome. I've got a feeling in my gut that more respite will be needed. All we can ask for is a better outcome than what is happening now.

I am not overly happy with what the nursing home is doing. There are several grey areas which we have told the administration about and they're going to get on top of it.

The question is: am I prepared to take the chance? If I take her out for a week and gamble and that there will be no bed available if she must go back. Then we are stuck. We would then have to go through all the bullshit of trying to find a home for her. As I said, this one is close by. It takes me ten minutes to get there. Anything else we're looking at a minimum of half an hour. It seems a shame that we must decide my wife's future; it sure does suck.

Okay, two weeks are up. We have to make the decision. Does she continue RESPITE, or do we take her home? This is what we have come up with: we have extended the respite for another two weeks. In the two weeks, if we want to, we can pull her out and take her home, or we'll see how she goes for the two-week period.

Went and paid a visit today. She was good in herself

but struggling to get out of the chair. Also in the room for the first time was a wheelchair and, in the bathroom, a lifting machine. This left so many questions unanswered, so we have tried to get the answers that we require. This is like trying to get blood out of a stone. I'm not a racist person, but every person, but two in that ward other than the patients are non-Australian, and some of them struggle to speak English. How the bloody hell can anyone communicate with them? The left hand does not know what the right hand is doing. I asked one of the nurses, "Is she able to get out of the chair on her own?" "Oh, yes." "Can she get off the toilet on her own?" "Oh, yes." "Can she get out of the bed on her own?" "Oh, yes." And then she says she's new, and this is the first time she's dealt with this patient. So in other words, she wouldn't have a bloody clue what is going on. I could not get a straight answer from anyone we asked; the so-called morning nurse was not available; the so-called afternoon nurse was also unavailable. The one in charge of the whole lot was not in today. At least, she is white, and you can talk to her. Surely, you would think she would be aware what it is going on in the joint. Also, you cannot run a nursing home the way they're doing it because of all this crap.

CHAPTER 15

It is now close to four weeks since she has been away from home. Just in case she's ready to come home, we have made some changes to her room. I wanted to purchase a hospital bed which will make life easier for her; we did not have enough funds in both our Old Age care packages and even if we did, I certainly did not want to pay $4,500 for a another new one. My old friend, eBay and marketplace, come in handy. We sourced out several which seemed suitable. We looked at a couple but as I have said before, some people that you deal with are fuck wits. To give you an example of the idiots you deal with, one guy had a bed for $1,000. He did not want to accept fund transfer to his bank, did not want me to give it to the delivery driver to give it to him. I explained that I am unable to get out to do any transactions and rely on other people to do it for me. He said he could not trust anybody else so the deal is off. What a dick.

We settled on a bed which was in Cranbourne. It was $1,500—new, only slept in once. His mother did not like it so they decided to sell. That's fine. I told him I was poor so could he knock the price down? He said he would leave the price as it is and delivered it for free. As mentioned before, there are different types of beds. This one is a single long, not as wide as mine, but a fraction longer. It does the same as what mine does. And he was right, it is as new— a mattress in perfect condition. The only thing wrong with this deal is they could not take the old mattress and base away. It looks like this will have to be a council job at a cost of $150. I also had to purchase two sets of single long-fitted sheets— one for the bed and one as a spare.

Now that I have purchased a hospital bed, my thoughts are that if we use the end where her head is to lift it up, this will enable her to sit up instead of having problems lifting herself up. At least, it will get her into the sitting position. This is an area that will help her get out of bed, I think. At least we can give it a try and not sit on our bums waiting to see what will happen. We will try and make things happen.

If we're looking to bring her home, we will need to get a patient transfer lifter or something which can lift her up and transfer her to another part of the house. The ones available through mobility care places must be operated by two people, are too big, and hard to use around the house. I purchased a patient transfer on eBay; it is a device which can help you lift the person up. This one is not like the hospital ones; it only needs one person to operate it. It is sitting in the box in the front room yet to be unpacked.

It states on the box the unit can be used four ways: (1) as a patient lifter; (2) as a small wheelchair; (3) a portable shower chair; and (4) as a portable commode chair. I'm waiting for someone strong to unpack it and assemble if necessary. It is a very heavy unit. I just hope it can be used inside by someone like me with weak muscle tone. At least we are prepared to give it a try at home and give her every chance of staying at home and keep her from going into permanent care.

We will see what happens in the next week that will give us an indication of where we're going.

As mentioned earlier, this is the only disease or medical problem that Jeanette has had. What a bastard of an illness to have. The poor bugger does not know what is going on. I really feel for her; she is now living in another world.

Remember when I went in and saw the neurologist and he told me I will be in a wheelchair within 10 years? I think he will be wrong. It will be less, I would say, between 12 and 18 months. Let's get the ball rolling now. The sooner I am able to purchase one, the better. My case manager had organised for a wheelchair professional to come out and show me some of the products in the range. In total, he bought four with him for me see. They ranged from small, easy to manoeuvre, inside up, to the larger outside machine.

First one I tried was the smallest. Certainly very nifty

and easy to handle. The starting price was $3,800. One problem though: I could not get out of it. It was far too low, and he had to help me out. I think we're going to have this problem with all your chairs. I just would not be able to get out of them. What I need is a vertical lift chair that will enable me to get out on my own. This has made his job a lot easier. Ordinary chairs are not an option; vertical lift chairs are the ones to look at. He did not have any with him, but he said go onto YouTube and you will find plenty up for discussion. The unit I would recommend is a Merits Dealer. They come in at around $5,800 but are on special now for Christmas at $4,900. I suggested he get one, bring it around, and give me a demonstration. He said he would have to order one in especially, and until he knows whether it is a definite sale or not, he could not do that until he knows the answer. I just said leave it at this stage, I'll get back to you.

 I did not mention to the wheelchair guy that I was sniffing around on the computer, checking out second-hand power wheelchairs. I was looking at eBay and Gumtree marketplace. There were plenty of wheelchairs available; many had outlived their usefulness, and many people were upgrading. It is up to the buyer to sort out the good from the bad. Trust me, there is a lot of bad and a lot of shit out there. I had a fair idea of what I was looking for. An ordinary manual wheelchair just would not do. With not having the strength in my arms, a manual wheelchair could not be pushed by me, so the only option is an electric chair. We have now also discovered that I cannot get out of an ordinary chair; it has to have the lifting option, so the one we are looking for is a full-power chair. This choice eliminated 80% of what was available. I thoroughly checked what was viable. Going through all the photos, there were very few powerchairs, and the ones that were there were knocked around a bit. Many of them would have to have been checked over by a wheelchair mechanic; some of them are in very ordinary condition. I finally came across a chair on eBay. It is amazing how you find so many cheap things for sale. When I see it, cheap lights start to flash, and the sign goes up. Buyer, beware. I also love a bargain. I am a big sucker for one and cannot resist if it is one.

A guy had a Quantum j623, supposing 18 months old and only used for six months. His sister used to have it. She does not need it any longer. I obtained this information from him by emailing back and forth. He probably thought I was a bloody nuisance, but I wanted to get to the nitty gritty of the deal.

His asking price was $750. First email was to ask if this product is still available which he replied "Yes, it was." The rest of the emails were just to confirm what condition the wheelchair was in and if it was still working, among other things. I emailed him explaining I was a pensioner doing it tough. I just had to buy a hospital bed and was a little short on funds. I will still have to find someone to deliver it to me, and if he would accept $600. He was only happy to help me out, and he said yes. I got his banking details and transferred the funds into his account. Usually, when you transfer funds into a new account, it will take four days to clear. He said once the funds are in the account, we could start the ball rolling. The funds did show that they were electronically transferred, and he was happy for all to go ahead immediately. He said, "Once you find somebody to deliver the unit, give him my number, and we will sort out when he can pick it up at a time which is suitable to both parties."

When you do business with people, you don't know that it can become very frustrating when you are trying to negotiate or deal with them and they do not get back to you. You sit and wait and wait for them to get back. They either couldn't care less, and they just do it in their time not worrying about you. I like to get the deal done and dusted and finalised as soon as possible; some people let the world just pass them by.

He lived a good hour away from me so any delivery driver will have to take this into account. Looked and found a driver who would pick it up and deliver it to me for $150. I was more than happy with the overall deal, the whole thing costing me $750.

After the delivery guy and the seller put their heads

together, it was agreed a ramp was needed to guide the chair into the van, and that two people were required to move it. The driver asked me if I could have somebody up my end to help take the chair off the van. I was more than grateful that he did not ask for extra to deliver because of the extra mucking around. It took the driver several days to pick the unit up and deliver it to me. I made sure that Shane was here with me when the chair was delivered. I did not believe an empty chair could be so heavy. It took both of the guys all their strength to get it inside. If at that time they knew how to use it, they could have just turned it on, press the control to go forward, and there you have it. Hindsight is a wonderful thing.

So, they wheeled it inside for its first inspection. I could not believe the condition the power chair was in; it looked brand new except one of the tyres had some mud on it. This chair has hardly been used and for him to sell it for $750, something must be wrong, but what?

We checked everything, looking for some fault. It was fully charged, and was ready to go. After every conceivable check, we found not a thing wrong and when it was booted up, it went like a beauty. I reckon it was a steal of the year. Spoke to Renee, our case manager, and told her what had happened. She checked the new price for me and through MobilityCare, the recommended retail price—you won't believe this—is $10,900. Well, it certainly is a change to kick a goal every now and then; it was one big goal here.

The chair is on the larger size than what we really wanted mainly for inside. I am quite sure it will not take me long in getting used to but once I know how to handle it, we hope all should be fine.

You won't believe this. The day after the wheelchair arrived, the president of the IBM association emailed me to let me know that a wheelchair with a lifting device was available in Williamstown for free. All I would have to do is check it out to see if it suited me and then organise for someone to go and pick it up and bring it back to Hastings. She sent photos, and the chair was in very good condition. I emailed back and told her that I just purchased a lifting chair and that to pass it on to someone else with IBM. That would really get some use out of it, but thank you all the same for thinking of me. I could have possibly used another chair just in case Jeanette needed one as she may in the future. Can't be greedy. I could have taken it, but that would have deprived somebody who needed a free chair. My motto: what goes around comes around.

It's now Sunday, the 11th of December 2022. Shane has just run me up to the nursing home to visit Jeanette. It is 3:00 o'clock in the afternoon, and she's still in her nightie when we arrived. She had had an accident in the bathroom. She did not quite make the toilet and the floor was in a mess. We do not know how long it had been there, but we had to notify the nurse of the mishap. Question: why was she still in her nightie at 3:00 o'clock? Has someone been there to dress her? Has anyone been there to check that she's okay in the toilet department? The biggest problem as mentioned, they would not have a bloody clue. That's it. She's coming home. I've decided. Next week, I will pull her out of the place and bring her home where she belongs. I am not going to let her become one of the zombie brigades. I will most certainly put everything down in writing, letting the establishment know of the happenings which have been going on. Surely, you would think that an establishment of that size would be a lot more professional in caring for patients. The actual company name is Full Care, and I believe they run up to eight different nursing homes in the state.

I will arrange for Jeanette to come home Tuesday or Wednesday of next week. I just cannot wave a magic wand and make it happen. Unfortunately, there is paperwork to be done to make it all official.

I think we're ready to have her home. We have the hospital bed, the patient transfer machine, and the wheelchair if needed. It's just a matter of setting everything up to make it all work. It certainly will be a busy couple of days organising carers and working out what days they will be needed. I still don't know if she can dress herself, what chairs or toilets she can get off of on her own. Anyway, we will find out soon enough; it will all be trial and error.

Finally put the patient transfer machine together and once someone is sitting in it, the unit becomes very heavy on a carpet. It is near impossible to move so I will have to put sheets of timber down temporarily and look at getting vinyl flooring in the bedroom. There is no other way around it.

Now that Jeanette is coming home, I have to make sure that we have enough funds in our home care package to pay for all this. Just going through it all—I know I have complained before—this is bloody ridiculous. Let me give you the rundown on this lot. Let's look at it individually. I am on a Level 3 package that entitles me to $35,138 per year care. The administrators take off the top $18,838, which leaves me with $16,900 a year. That averages out at five hours per week at $65 an hour. Jeanette's package is the same. The other part that pisses me off is out of the $65 an hour, they take another $34 per hour, so out of the $35,138, they end up taking $27,078, which leaves a grand old total of $8,060 for the client; that is just hard to believe.

This will definitely mean I will have to get outside help. At this stage, I believe we will need somebody in every morning, seven days a week, to dress, and four days to shower her. This is where the nursing home needs a good kick up the arse for not letting us know if she can get out of chairs. We have to know if she's capable of going to bed on her own and moving around the house.

There is a mob called Mapel. Once you're registered, you can hire carers at a lower rate. This rate must be negotiated with the carer and then Mapel takes 10% off the top. All I must do is work out how many hours they will be needed over and above the normal.

This is unbloody believable. Just found out that Home care also uses Mapel and that they take 10% of what you pay them. I do not know if they negotiate the fee or I negotiate the fee. I will certainly find that out. Again, you can bet that they negotiate the fee and it will be is high as what they normally charge. I certainly will fill you in.

I've just had a meeting with the big boss of the nursing home. Her name is Petra. She had asked to see me after I had put in a complaint about the treatment of Jeanette or the lack of treatment. Whatever. She was very concerned as were we. She apologised that the treatment that Jeanette received was not up to standard. The excuse she used for why Jeanette was still in her nightie at 3:00 p.m. was that she had run out of normal clothes to wear. They were all in the wash. I mentioned that this was unlikely as she had four tops, three bottoms, as well as under clothes. I doubt if all of them are in the wash. At once, she was also surprised that she had as many clothes as she did. She agreed that it would be highly unlikely that this was the case; she would investigate this further. Regarding the faeces on the bathroom floor, she explained that the cleaner was not available that weekend and that the nurses had to fill in and do the job.

Petra also explained to us that many members of the team are new and are being trained by Australian staff. Many of the new staff are Indian, and their communication skills do not exist. They cannot explain in proper English what is happening and what they're doing with the patients. They are trying to get on top of this so that it makes life a lot simpler.

CHAPTER 16

I have arranged with Petra to take Jeanette out of the home on Wednesday of next week. She has agreed to keep the room open for a period of one week just in case things don't work out as planned at home. As mentioned earlier, I have everything in place for her arrival, can't wait. Under normal circumstances, the home is unable to hold a room. If the home has an enquiry, they just can't turn that enquiry away. We were most probably lucky that they had several spare rooms free, so making the room available was possible. All they did was not fill in the paperwork that Jeanette had gone; no one was the wiser.

How excited am I? I'm like a boy waiting to get his train set for Christmas. I just can't wait to have her home. I'm going around telling all the neighbours that she will be home tomorrow. I have notified all my friends by telephone that she will be home tomorrow, I just can't wait. Everybody knows how anxious I am, and I hope that I don't fall flat on my arse, and it does not work.

The big day has arrived. Shane has picked me up and

we have arrived at the nursing home to pick my darling up and bring her home. As we arrive, she's sitting in her wheelchair, doing some colouring in. Shane has gone into her room to pack her bag. All is ready. Two nurses take her out to the car and ask her to stand up so that she could hop into the car. Do you think she would get up? No way, the nurses tried everything to entice her to stand without any success. At any stage that the nurses tried to touch her, all hell broke loose. She verbally abused both ladies. She said, "Get your hands off me! Don't touch me, leave me alone." She also started to get a little physical by pushing her hands towards the girls. I looked at Shane, Shane looked at me. We had never seen her like this. Shane decided to walk around to the wheelchair and physically lift her up and plonk her into the front seat of the car. She carried on, "Let me go, let me down." But it did fall on deaf ears.

Stage one…done! Have we made the correct decision? We can still change our minds. No. Let's continue.

It is only a short drive to our place—about 10 minutes. There has been no reaction on Jeanette's face as she arrives home. Now, the fun starts at this end. We entice her to get out of the car and again, she was very reluctant to do so. We virtually had to physically drag her out towards her walker. Talk about fun. It took her at least 20 minutes to walk from the car to the front door. Every step she took you would have thought she had been shot. Step, moan, step, moan, step, moan. We asked if she was in pain in any certain place. She just said that it hurt every time she took a step. It turned out that the legs were sore. I would say it would come down to the lack of exercise she's not getting at the nursing home. Not once have I seen anybody walking with her therefore, she's just not getting the exercise and walking that she needs to keep her mobile. Finally, she had made it inside. Halfway into the bedroom, she stalls and says to me, "I want to go to the toilet." I said, "Five steps and you are there." She politely said, "Don't worry, I am doing it now." And she did. We are learning very quickly what she can and can't do.

Oh my God! What have we got ourselves into? She continued to do what she had to do—standing up five steps from the toilet. "We are in great trouble. There is no way that she is going to let us touch her so that we can clean her up. What the fuck are we going to do?" We suggested to her to move herself into the bathroom so that we could start to clean things up. There is no way she even wanted to move. We could not get her to take one step. Do you believe in miracles? I think I do now, you would not believe what happened. At this crisis point, our case manager, Renee, decided to come over to see how we were getting on. She was more than interested in what the outcome of this will be. She walked in asking what's going on. I replied, "We are in a heap of trouble. She has stalled and has done number two's." "Well we'd better clean it up then." She walked over to Jeanette spoke to her very calmly, and Jeanette moved into the toilet. Renee was able to change her. Thank goodness. She was wearing pull-ups which caught everything. All the cleaning gear was already there. Also at that time, another carer arrived, and they both did what had to be done to make her respectable. What a relief it is! Good to have people who know what they're doing around you all was back to being well. So we thought.

My wheelchair finally come in handy. Renee said it would be easier to move Jeanette in a wheelchair than to get her to use her walker. Renee certainly had a ball trying to work out how to drive the chair. Jeanette got the ride of her life with Renee driving. In the very short time that she was there, we learned the important aspects of what she can do and can't do at home. And if the nursing home did not have their heads up their bums, they could've supplied us with this information before we tried it out ourselves. So, the experiment of bringing the boss home has most certainly backfired. Everything that we wanted to work has not worked at all, so it is back to the drawing board.

In this short period of over a couple of hours, we've learned that she is unable to get in and out of a car without help. She can't stand with the aid of a walker. Also, she is unable to walk. Once she's standing, a wheelchair is the only option. It does not matter what chair it is. She needs help getting out of it which includes getting off the toilet. I have come to the conclusion that having her at home is no longer an option. Unfortunately, permanent care is the only thing available to us.

One of the huge problem areas is she keeps fighting the person who is trying to help her get on or off the chair. It could lead to physical violence; verbal violence is not uncommon. We were able to have a very good and fruitful discussion of what were our options. We were all able to see firsthand what she was capable of, which was not a lot, and everybody reached the same conclusion. Sorry, my love, a nursing home is the only option. The vote was 5-0.

Now that we have her sitting in the wheelchair, how do we get her back to the nursing home? We are aware of the difficulties we will have, trying to get her into the car. Someone has come up with the suggestion to contact one of the taxi cabs companies and use the wheelchair taxi. The chair is fitted with the correct safety points which you need when in one of these cabs. This could be very interesting as that is what we will be looking to do at a later date when I am unable to drive. Just being an ordinary person, I thought the procedure would be quite straightforward in ordering one of these. This is what we found out after contacting the company. They had to find out if they had any of these taxi cabs available as the normal procedure is to book them in the morning so that they have got a full load for the day. After ringing backwards and forwards for over an hour, there is none available for the day. I found this to be ordinary for anybody who needs one of these taxis. You would think there would be more available. Not everybody can plan their day ahead just in case of an emergency.

I was happy and satisfied in my own mind that I had done everything I possibly could to bring her home. We had to try it and now, I'm 100% convinced that she has to stay in a nursing home full-time. I'm not happy but there was no other option.

Thank goodness that two Home care carers were available to help us out on the day. Without them, we would've had a problem. Everyone helped everyone get her into the car, and she was driven back to the nursing home. Shane had telephoned ahead and there were two nurses waiting with a wheelchair as we pulled up. I saw Petra in the office. By the time I had finished, Jeanette got herself settled and she was doing some colouring in when I arrived. I said, "Are you having a good day? You look as if you're very comfortable there." Her reply was, "Yeah, very happy. Having a good time." It is as if nothing had happened in the last hour and a half to two hours. Totally convinced you are home now.

This certainly has come as a surprise. Four weeks ago, she was admitted to the hospital, thinking that it could be a UTI infection that was knocked on the head, and the conclusion was the dementia is getting worse. The hospital would not let her home under any circumstances. If there is no one there to look after her, she had to go into a minimum of two weeks respite that turned out to be three weeks, and now, that has turned out to be permanent care. It is marvellous how things change in a small period of time. So after 54 years, I am now on my own. One thing I'm grateful for is that I'm not in a grieving period. Or so I thought. It is not as if she has just died. She is 10 minutes away, so I can see her daily if I wish.

By golly, you do not realise the amount of paperwork and red tape that we must go through to change everything over. In the government's eyes, we are now a single couple—now separated, so that means that the pensions will change from being a double to two singles. Centrelink must be notified for any changes to our income, even though they're making the changes, silly, but I have to inform them of the changes they're making to our accounts. Also, being on the wrong side of the government will make your life pure hell. Cross your tees and dot your dots and everything will be hunky dory. Here, we have another arithmetic lesson to have. Somebody in full care means the patient must pay an amount of $56.87 per day or $796.48 per fortnight with the present rates. A person on a double pension gets $773.80 per fortnight. As you can see, the double pension is not enough to cover the cost of full care.

The single pension rate is $1,026.50 per fortnight. They take out $796.48, leaving you with a grand old sum of $230.02. At least, it does not leave us out of pocket. They require you to do a means test to show that you have not got as much money as you say you have. Again, all red tape but it has to be done. I feel we've done everything right. Time will tell once the pension cheques start coming in. There is sure to be some stuff up somewhere along the line.

The nursing home needs some assurance that they will not be out of pocket so during the signing of the contracts, they are given a guarantee by either me or my son that the full amount owed will be paid by us at any given time so if the government go broke and are unable to pay, the onus falls back onto us two. What a load of bullshit. There is a small amount of 67 pages which make up the bullshit. Shane said to me that he would fill the forms out. He can do it a lot faster. My main concern was he fills it out correctly so there is no comeback by Centrelink or the nursing home.

The ordinary bloke on the street does not know how the Aged Care system works and does not want to know until he's ready to go look at it himself. He will then find it mind-boggling. Not in my wildest dreams did I think it was as sophisticated as it seems it is. I think it depends on what end you are looking at it from. I will run through it so that the ordinary bloke will understand what I'm talking about. If you have a loved one ready to go into a nursing home, you have two choices and that is you either pay for it or you don't. Simple! If you are a couple, one can go in on the free list (government pays). The other must pay. In my case, Jeanette goes into a nursing home on her own. No assets, does not have to pay. The pension goes to a single rate and the nursing home takes roughly 85% of your pension, with nothing else to pay. The only out-of-pocket expenses will be any medicinal scripts through the chemist and any personal items which you may need.

Now it is a different case for the spouse, like me. If I chose to or had to go into a home, circumstances are totally different. The house or unit which I own are classed as assets, therefore, the room in the home would have to be paid for. The nursing home values the room at $450,000 buy in. Simple as this. Give me a returnable deposit of $450,000. We invested at 6% getting $27,000 in interest per annum, either one or the other. If you have the spare cash, there's no need to sell your assets. All nursing homes in the state of Victoria operate on the same system. The rooms vary in price, ranging from $450,000 up to $900,000. It all depends on what assets you have and to what room you would purchase.

In my case, once I have to go into a nursing home, I will have no choice but to put my property on the market so that I can come up with the funds that they require as I do not have a spare $30,000 a year to give to them.

What does annoy me about the whole system is that if I buy in at $450,000 a year and I live 10 years at the end of that period, my next of kin still only gets $450,000. The property itself could have doubled in value alone. When you weigh it all up, I do not suppose there are too many options available. One small consolation is that the money is guaranteed to be there after the 10 years or more.

Once a person is admitted into full care at a nursing home, the package that the government gives ceases. So, any funds which have accumulated in Jeanette's account get lost back to the government. Unfortunately, they cannot be used in any other area. In the past, they could rob Peter to pay Paul. In other words, use one account against the other so that was the plans were made to be flexible. Oh well good while it lasted.

Well, well, after 54 years, the journey is finally over. My darling wife Jeanette, due to her rotten dementia, has left me. She had nothing to do with the decision-making anyway. There is no way known that I could have helped her at home any longer. I feel so empty and lost without her by my side. I would never ever worry where she was as I knew she was in the house somewhere and after a few steps, I would be by her side. Unfortunately, that no longer can happen. It is like losing someone who has died. At least, I can see her whenever I want to as the nursing home is only 10 to 15 minutes away.

CHAPTER 17

One area where the doctors are always concerned is the ability I have to fall easily. Unfortunately, with IBM, this seems to be a common occurrence. I have noted many times while writing this book the number of falls that I have had and the amount of close calls that I've had. I find it very important to list any falls that I have. On Wednesday, the 21st of December 2022, I felt I had the most significant fall as yet. I was standing in the kitchen, looking down. I saw a drinking straw on the ground. Instead of getting the gadget to pick things up, I stupidly bent down to pick it up and yes, you guessed it, arse over I went. I landed on both knees and with the motion going forward ended up on my ribs on the right-hand side. I was unable to put my arms in front of me to cushion the fall. Pain-wise, this has been the worst I have had. There was a career in the room at the time. She heard me fall and certainly heard my moans and groans. She tried to lift me. No hope. I just said to her, "Leave me be. I will try and get up on my own as you will not be able to lift me." She offered to call an ambulance, which I declined. They are so busy now that my call would only be a nuisance call. I was flat on my stomach. The pain was in my knees and my ribs. I lay on the ground for at least 15 minutes while waiting for the pain to subside.

I could not stand up. I did not even try because I know I cannot get up anyway, so I have attempted to crawl on injured knees into the bedroom very slowly. I have difficulty holding myself up with my wonky forearms. I don't think they're designed to hold my whole body weight; that makes crawling a lot more difficult. I finally got into the bedroom where we lowered the hospital bed to the bare minimum so that I could climb on. Man, oh man, slowly I was able to climb up onto the bed which we then lifted up and I was able to stand. From the time I fell to the time I stood up in the bedroom, nearly 40 minutes had passed—certainly a slow process. Any carer who has a person fall while they are on duty must report the incident to head office immediately so within 40 minutes or so, they were informed of the incident. I did not think a lot about it, it was just another fall to me as I thought at that time. The body suffered minimally, only a small graze on each knee. I did not even warrant a band aid. They insisted that I go to the doctor to have a report of the incident. I felt it would only be a pain in the bum at this stage. Also, any visit to the doctors would only benefit them and nobody else, so I put it on the back burner and did not go.

Come Monday, 28th of December, I was taking Bo for a walk. I was using my walker. I was very aware that one of the neighbours has a German shepherd which was running around loose. My main concern was that this dog did not gang up on Bo. I was looking to where the dog was. What I was not aware of was the neighbour—his name turned out to be Tyler—had already put the dog away without me knowing that the danger had passed and Bo was safe. Me worrying about the dog situation, was not concentrating on what I was doing while walking with the walker (as I have mentioned before, I must think before I take steps), and the inevitable happened. Over I go again. As usual, I can feel this happening and knowing what is going to happen yet, I still cannot do anything about it. I just let nature take its course this time. I went down on my knees and my feet. The bloody fall alarm which I am wearing deliberately each time I walk did not register that a fall had taken place. I did not go to ground fast enough, so here I am on the ground, blood pissing out at both knees. I smashed the alarm onto the ground and it finally worked. It was able to contact Shane and others on the list. I was able to talk to him to let him know the situation, while the neighbours who were fantastic attended to my situation. Several came to my aid to make sure that I was all right. Once they knew I would be okay and had contacted relatives, they relaxed a little. Sue, who is a retired nurse, attended to the grazes on my knees, cleaning them up with antiseptic and placing band-aids over the wounds.

You certainly find out that once you are in a pickle, help is very close by. Several people including Tyler who I had mentioned earlier as well as Stephen George, who is one of our new body corporate committee members, heard the commotion while on his daily walk. They both waited till I was steady enough, helped me to my feet, and escorted me to the unit. Steven and Sue waited with me in the unit until Shane arrived. Once they knew everything was fine, they then left us on our own. Isn't getting old fantastic?

My knees had been attended to, thanks to Sue. Also, the toe next to the big toe on my left foot took a beating. I think the pain is indicating that it could be broken. I have mentioned before that many toes have been broken in the past; the only other thing that was hurting was my pride. One of my main thoughts was that I did not land on my ribs. That would have been a disaster.

I have reached the conclusion that me using the walker other than making me more balanced is just a waste of time as it does not help me when I fall. I have not got the muscle mass in the arms to hold me up when I know I'm falling. I will continue to use it as it does give me a little more confidence when I walk.

All the fuss is over, everyone has gone home. They all checked that I was comfortable and safe sitting here on my own. I assured them that everything was fine, so here am I sitting at the kitchen bench with aches on top of my aches. Getting off the subject just a little, as you know I'm verbally talking to the computer, and it is writing down what I say. I just had a little giggle where I read out about aches on top of aches, the computer put down eggs on top of eggs. Anyway, I thought it was quite funny. It does not rain but it pours. I am having a new sensation occur where I had fallen on my ribs the week before and not suffering any significant pain. Suddenly, the pain started to be unbearable. I was able to get some pain relief to help the situation, but they did very little.

As it turned out, I must have dislodged something on the right-hand side with the last fall, so I thought about calling an ambulance. The ambulance people advised us that they were so busy, it would be easier to drive into emergency yourself. It came up in conversation amongst ourselves that if we go into Frankston Public Hospital, the wait could be quite substantial—very easily up to 12 hours as they do get very busy there. Unfortunately, the normal public are brainless and go to a public hospital with a sore toe instead of using their local GP. Therefore, it clogs up the system for genuine people. One of my neighbours suggested we go into Peninsula Private Hospital, pay a premium fee to be seen by one of their doctors. If it is anything real serious and you must be admitted, that would have to be worked out at a later date as you do not have private cover. Also, the wait would be much less than the other alternative. They will not be as busy and you will be seen much quicker.

So we pay the $400 premium which covered X-rays and seeing a doctor. Waited for 45 minutes. They did a CT scan and the technician said the results of the scan should only take an hour.

We waited for over three hours for the final results when a doctor was kind enough to relay them to us.

Guess what? Seven broken ribs later—not bruised, all broken—but not displaced. The report reads 4th, 5th, 6th, 7th, 8th, 9th, and 10th.

The doctor said, "Boy, you don't muck around, do you? If you're going to do something, you must do it properly and you most certainly did. My advice is total rest and pain management for you to get over this. Go to the emergency department of Frankston Public Hospital, and we will organise for you to be admitted through that system." The doctor then said this, "There is no way that I would let my 76-year-old father with broken ribs go home." The doctor then organised the paperwork and a letter for me to take into Frankston. The doctor said it could be up to a three-week recovery time, maybe more as each case is different. "Can I go home and collect a couple of things first?" The doctor said, "No way, go straight into emergency. They are expecting you so that you can be admitted virtually straight away." The doctor gave us the letter and we proceeded to leave the hospital. I said to Shane, "Go straight home. I want to get a couple of things." "But Dad, he said to go straight in." I said, "Go home first." Very reluctantly, he headed into the home direction. On the way, I said to him, "Who is going to look after the animals?" He said, "I can probably give them the odd day as I have to work. They will be okay on their own for a few days here and there." My answer to that was, "You have just made up my mind. I will not go to the hospital as the animals need looking after. They're not used to being on their own. They will most certainly fret if no one is there. Anyway, I don't need a hospital to get rest. I can get that by staying home. Imagine me in the hospital, just lying there supposedly resting. No fucking way. I will be better off at home."

I have never been a hospital person. If there's nothing wrong with me, in other words if I'm able to walk around in the hospital, I should be able to walk around at home. So the decision was made, I am staying home. Also, if I went into hospital, I would worry about the animals so much that I would not be able to rest. I will be much better and more rested in my own home. I telephoned the hospital and ask to speak to the doctor who had made the decision; he was not there so I just left a message stating that I would not be taking his advice and would not proceed to the hospital and left it at that. All I had to get under control was the pain management. I will ring Doctor Kelly in the morning.

Shane promised the neighbours who helped me that he would contact them as soon as he had some news. When we arrived home, he started to ring them one by one and explained to them the decision Dad had made. They all agreed I would be better off at home to get my rest. Have decided to leave the front door unlocked. The amount of people coming in and out reminds you of a very busy city street. "No need to knock, just come straight in." Was easier than getting up each time the doorbell rang. Won't be getting too much rest at this rate, would prefer them here than not here. Very considerate of them.

Sure, one of my lovely neighbours must have shit the bed as bright and early as 7:30 a.m., she thought that everybody would have been up as she was only interested in whether I had had breakfast or a cup of coffee, and was generally looking after myself. She offered to go down to the medical clinic and drop off a copy of the letter that the doctor had given us the night before, explaining the injuries I had suffered. As soon as my doctor had come in, she would be given a copy of the letter and would know what's going on. At around about 9:20 a.m., Doctor Kelly rang me. She had read the letter and offered to organise some pain relief. I asked her if she could organise a mobile nurse to come around to my house and treat my knee injuries, changing the dressings every couple of days. This she said she could do.

As it turned out, the Royal District Nursing Service had been taken over by a new company and informed us that our request had been denied because of a lack of personnel in our area. "So we're very sorry but you are on your own." Too bad if I had a major injury which needed treating daily. I've been treating injured knees for years so I can do it myself very easily. I will have to be careful of my toe next to the big toe on my left leg which is very inflamed, more than likely broken I have some antibiotics which I will take to treat it so it does not get infected.

Talking about pain relief, Kelly has now got me on the 20-milligram patch which seems to be helping big time with the pain in the arms and shoulders. Also a big thing that I have noticed is, I have restarted on the OSTERINE that Phil makes. Have been back on it for about two weeks and I have noticed the pain in my hands, arms, and shoulders has disappeared. I am now totally convinced that the OSTERINE works along with the other medication that has been prescribed for me. She has also given me Endone to help with the ribs.

Another chapter has come to an end. My driving has ended after doing something stupid which has made me come to this sensible decision. There is a tomato farm about six kilometres from where we live and me, being a tomato lover, decided to take the plunge and drive for the first time in a long time and get some tomatoes. As I may have mentioned earlier, my biggest problem with the car is getting out using my arms to push myself out. It seems to be getting harder each time I try to do it. On arrival, I turned the ignition off and proceeded to get out. Do you think I could get out? I tried every way possible and I just could not get out. I turned myself around and tried to back out and with my strong legs, I went to ground. Big mistake. I was finally out of the car but now I could not get up. I tried everything I knew to lift both my legs up at the same time. Without luck, I was able to get one leg up onto the car floor but the other one I just could not lift. It took me 25 minutes of tooting the horn to try and get someone's attention and me trying to get into the car. Anyway, I finally made some headway and was able to stand up. Now that I was up, I had to try the tomatoes out for the first time in a long time. The tomatoes were rubbish. He has put the prices up from $3 per 700 grammes to $5 per 700 grammes. I don't think his sales are as good as they used to be. The product is sitting there longer and going off quicker as these ones were nowhere near the quality that they used to be. Time will tell. He has lost me now.

The drive home took around 10 minutes. I must admit I had trouble holding and turning the steering wheel. On arrival, I paid more attention on getting out this time so I would not be stuck. I achieved the goal of getting out safely for the last time. I know I have said it before, but this is the last time I will drive. Well, trust me, this is definitely the last time I will drive. I then decided to sell the car as I had no use for it any longer.

I contacted a couple of car dealers, told them what I had, and what I wanted. One decided to come around that same day to appraise the vehicle. I decided to do it this way and not muck around getting a roadworthy certificate and have the car detailed. I maybe could have gotten a couple of grand more, but this way, there's no stuffing around. The dealer and I reached an amicable amount which was paid into my account. The next day and the day after that, they picked the car up to do what they had to do with it. It turned out to be a very quick sale. I was happy as the car was 14 years old. It had low K's but was still 14 years old. I find it amazing how much rubbish you have in the glove box and even the electronics under the seat. I think I can just about open a shop selling KFC towelettes. I passed on my disabled sticker to which I just recently renewed and should last several years to Shane to use when he drives me to wherever he has to. That will definitely come in handy for him. Just recently, the councils decided to have a clampdown on the fake disability stickers which appeared on car windscreens. The fines for fake ones were quite substantial.

CHAPTER 18

I thought it's quite appropriate to bring up one of my major loves in my life—the animals. Throughout our 54 years of married life, there's not been a period where we have not had any animals in the house—mainly dogs, cats, fish, birds, you name it. We've had it, so to speak. I did mention earlier briefly that I wrote a book. This was done in 2012 and was published through an American firm called Xlibris, a self-publishing company. We had spent $15,000 on the production and marketing of the book. After several run-ins with them after the marketing procedures did not work for the third time because everything they did created no sales, we finally gave them the flick and handed over the publishing to another company called Book Trail Agency. They also proved to be as useless as tits on a bull. I did not mention the name of the book. It was called *The Gold-Plated Dog*. After we went to book trial, we decided to change the name of the book to *Roscoe, the Gold-Plated Dog*. Again, after several failed marketing attempts, I did not have to give them the flick. My contacts became uncontactable.

Anytime I emailed, there was no reply. I sent an email to the head office stating the copyright has been handed to someone else.

After 10 odd years trying to get this bloody book marketable—so maybe another two or $3,000 spent—maybe we can get something out of the wreck. We now have Great Writers Media as our publisher. We have changed the book around, totally adding five more chapters, changing the title to *Our Dogs* plus *Roscoe, the Gold-plated Dog*. It has 20 more photos; finished product has 225 pages. Let's hope this mob can do something with it. The original idea was not to publish the book. It was just to keep me active while the dog was going through his problems. The main story tells how as animal lovers, we spent over $30,000 keeping Rosco alive and mobile. Over a period of the last 10 years, publishing the book has been nothing but a pain in the bum, and I would never go through it again. There are so many persons with small companies that are out there to rip you off. There is an old saying: once bitten, twice shy.

At this present moment, we only have three animals of our own, plus we have an additional wild group which we feed and that is the ringtail possums. They come around nightly, and I give them a feed of one pear cut into quarters plus five biscuits. They are not tame, but I still get some enjoyment in feeding and watering them.

Our cat's name is Oscar, a male medium-haired ginger

pussy who is six years of age, very lovable as cats can be, and very bossy towards our dog Bo. During the evening, I usually lock him in the front room as if he is left out. His favourite trick is to start meowing before daybreak, waking up the whole household. Once he is locked up, he seems quite happy to sleep right. Through this way, everybody gets a good night's sleep.

A very small part of our family is a very large silver shark. I have had him for over 12 years, and he is close to a foot long. He lives alone in a three-feet tank; he seems quite happy on his own.

The major member of my family is a toy poodle cross named Bo. In April this year—it is now February—he will turn 12 years of age. He is my baby and I absolutely adore him. I love them all, but Bo holds a special place. At that time, we purchased two dogs, one we named Ozzy and the other Bo. Unfortunately, Ozzy passed away from organ failure 18 months ago. Talk about getting a kick in the guts. That was a major one. I decided to continue with Bo on his own as it is too bloody painful to keep going through losing animals. Bo now is suffering from two major ailments—one being a heart murmur and the other is kidney problems. He goes around the house coughing regularly. The heart murmur causes the coughing, but if we treat to stop the coughing, it will affect the kidneys. So unfortunately, the coughing we must put up with. He's on a special tablet which treats the kidney disease as well as the heart. The vet has given him a new tablet to stop the coughing without any success. Due to these ailments, he is on a special kidney food. It is imported from the USA and it costs $6.50 per 370 gramme. Can be pretty expensive stuff. I buy 12 at a time from pet stock. They deliver once every three weeks. It is what they call an automatic order.

Naturally, all the animals rely on me. If not for me, they don't survive. They get spoiled rotten. One of the treats I buy both the dog and cat is a special freeze-dried chicken breast. It comes in at $55 per 200 grammes. I give them a couple of pieces each per day. They would eat the whole packet at once if they could. I take Bo for a walk daily and after the walk, that is when the treats come out. Oscar seems to know exactly when to come into the bedroom to get his share. My motto is: you don't have them for a long time. While I have them and I can afford it, I will give them the best available. I know by the way both the cat and dog look at me that they love me. They want to be with me, and I love every bit of it. Bring it on guys.

It has always been one of my main concerns. If I were to leave this place, how do the animals cope on their own? This is why I'm always very reluctant to go to the hospital in case you are kept overnight or even longer. Once again, I'm a very lucky person to have Shane as my son. He does pay attention to what I do when I feed the animals. Also, he stayed here when I was in the hospital with my heart attack. That time, he knew what to do with the animals and nothing much has changed except for the medication, so he knows that the possums have to be fed as well as the fish. Even though I am concerned, I know in my own mind that he will do a good job and look after the animals, so really, I'm worrying about nothing.

We have now entered the year 2023. It is the 23rd of January. The last couple of weeks have been rather interesting. While sitting at the kitchen bench, I started to feel nauseous and it reached the stage where I had to lay down. I did not actually chuck up but it felt like I wanted to. Normally, if I ever feel this way, I stick my finger down my throat and make myself vomit. I feel better that way. You could not believe this, but with the toilet being raised, I have to hang on with both hands if I want to stick my head into the bowl. So if I take one hand away to stick down my throat, I tend to fall over due to my lack of balance. Bloody IBM gets into everything.

I speak to Doctor Kelly on a regular two-week basis as the patch she prescribes only contains two patches which last two weeks. Therefore, I need to renew the prescription fortnightly. On the Wednesday, she calls, and I tell her about the nausea. She said, "If it is the same tomorrow, contact me, and we will do something about it." Tomorrow came around with no change in my condition, so we contacted the surgery, and I told the receptionist that Kelly said to ring. That did not make any difference to her. She insisted that I see another doctor. I was not prepared to do that, so I just hung up. We were able to get onto a new service where you contact a doctor by phone. They speak to you and if a script is needed, they will send it to your phone. We did that. He organised a script for nausea which we had filled. After several hours, we had found that they did not work. I'm still as crook as a dog and continued to rest myself on the bed. It has now entered its third day and all I want to do is lie down as that is the only thing that seems to ease the condition. Each time I get up, all I want to do is chuck. As I had not eaten, there's nothing to bring up. I said to Shane, "I can't go on with this any longer. I'm going to call an ambulance to see if they can do something." The ambulance arrived within the hour and after an examination, they decided to take me to the hospital. Seeing that this was lingering on, they asked me which hospital I would prefer and after Jeanette's encounter with Rosebud Hospital, that is where I decided to go. The ambulance people checked to see if there were any vacancies there, which we were lucky that there were. It took at least half an hour drive to get there. It was not just the nausea that they were concerned about but also the seven cracked ribs. That seems to have a large bearing on them taking me to the hospital. The paramedic stated that it is very hard to treat cracked ribs especially at home as you do not rest enough. The only treatment is rest, and at home, you keep aggravating the ribs which means it takes a lot longer to heal. A few days in hospital equals to at least two weeks at home.

Upon arrival, it is the same as what happens on TV. The ambulance paramedics tell the hospital nurses what problems there seem to be. At this stage, we do not know if the hospital was even going to admit me. So, the initial examination was done by the nurses and all the information naturally gets passed on to the doctors. After several hours in the emergency department, getting prodded and poked at, they decided that I was bad enough to be admitted to a medical ward. I was quite happy to be put into the hospital as I did really feel like shit.

Me being the tightwad that I am, my mobile phone comes with $50 a year plan. It is only used in case of an emergency. If I use the phone to ring anyone, the fees are astronomical, so I get everyone to ring me. Text calls are fine; they are affordable. Once I knew I was being admitted, I texted Shane to let him know and ask him to bring me some clothes and also to allow a couple of days before he came down so that they can hopefully find out what is the matter with me.

I appreciate what the people in the hospitals do for you, and their main aim is to get you well. The whole environment is degrading. Over the years, I've had my share of hospital food. I have yet to come across a hospital which serves palatable meals. The food here was exactly the same; all the meals are sourced from outside the hospital. The best part of the nightly meal was the soup, especially the mushroom—very delicious. On one occasion, I saw mushroom soup was on the menu and I ordered two soups and no mains. The orange juice and the ice cream are also nice. Otherwise, the rest is bland and tasteless. Being a type 2 diabetic also made a difference in what they would serve me. One thing I have noticed is the nurses will not eat the hospital food that the patients get served up. I wonder why. Maybe they know something that we don't. To help fill in with the meals is the little packet of biscuits they bring around. One is served with cheese and crackers; the other is two sweet biscuits on their own. I would ask the nurses if they could find me a little pack of vegemite that I could use with the cheese and crackers. I used this quite often to help fill in a void which existed between meals. Why do hospitals serve up stews and sloppy meat dishes? Me being the fussy eater that I am would starve if I had to rely on hospital food…yuck!

Hospitals don't only supply the treatment you need to get better but are also excellent in providing the right people to talk to help get over some of your problems, such as social workers, OTs, dietitians, and physios. They offered all this to me and I naturally said yes to them all. The more, the merrier to help me get over some of the mental problems I was going through.

The first night, the doctor on duty and I had a talk for about an hour. The subject covered was what has happened to me in the last month. All in all, it seems to be an accumulation of different things that had been going on. He said, "You have had a lot on your plate with the IBM. Dealing with that on its own is not easy. Having a fall and breaking seven ribs are also not easy. Then your wife of only 54 years gets herself put into full care. You do not realise this but you are going through a grieving period. Now you come down with nausea to top everything off. Put them all together, no wonder you feel the way you feel." He strongly suggested that I speak to the persons made available to help me.

The dietitian came around and said I am lacking in protein, so I was prescribed a chocolate milk drink, 50 millilitres a time, four times a day. "I don't know about you, but I know that if I'm feeling nauseous and I have a milk drink, I feel a bloody darn site worse." That idea lasted two drinks. I then refused to take anymore. The dietitian was told of my decision so she organised a fruit protein drink. Have never been able to stand apple juice. Guess what flavour the protein drink was. You guessed it, one mouth full and that ended up in the bin. On the final day, I met another dietitian and told her about the apple juice and the chocolate drink. She agreed with me that most of this stuff tasted revolting. She suggested that I try Sustagen when I get home and flavour it to my own taste. "That is the answer to any of the problems you are having."

The third night at around 2:30 a.m., I was lying in bed unable to sleep and just thinking as well as feeling sorry for myself. The nausea was still very prevalent; the nurses and doctors had failed in that area at this stage. I was talking to myself and had realised that I was in this great big rut. I said to myself, "For God's sake Wayne, stop feeling sorry for yourself. There is plenty to live for. Jeanette is still alive, and you can see her every couple of days, even every day if you want to. There are thousands of people living on their own. At least, you still have the dog and cat but they will not survive without you, so get up off your arse stop feeling sorry for yourself and make it happen." That is exactly what I needed—a little bit of motivation from myself. When I awoke after finally getting to sleep, my attitude seemed to change, had breakfast, had a shower, and even went for a walk around the hospital with the help of a nurse of course. The nurses were very impressed after I told them that I had to kick myself up the bum to get myself moving.

From that moment, everything seemed to change, mainly my attitude towards what was happening in the place. I saw the doctor and he said the main reason you are nauseous is the medication you have been on. You still have the pain patch and we have stopped you using Endone; the combination of the two is enough to make anyone nauseous, so the medication we are using for your ribs is the basic Panadol. That will be all you require. You will notice a change in the nausea very soon. I told the doctor what I had done that morning. He was very impressed and said that seeing your attitude had changed and that we finally found out what is causing your problem, if everything goes well, we may let you go home tomorrow. Sometimes, doctors leave a lot to be desired. I told them right from the start that I was taking Endone along with the patch, so really, it should not have taken them four days to find out what the problem was. It was staring at him right in the face, right from the start. Anyway, it is what it is.

That afternoon, I was fortunate enough to talk to a social worker. She was very interested in what was going on as well. The same as the doctor earlier, we went through everything. She agreed with the doctor that I'm going through a grieving period. One of her main concerns was how I am going to cope being home alone, who is going to prepare meals, who is going to bathe me, how independent am I on my ow, all these personal questions. She said, "I cannot let you leave the hospital unless you have a personal plan organised for when you get home. My main concern is you and I have a duty of care to make sure that you get it right." The doctor and the social worker must have put their heads together because he came back that afternoon and virtually said the same as she did: have yourself a plan and you can go home.

I relayed all that was said to Shane and he, in turn, relayed it all to Renee, our case manager. It was up to her to come up with a plan that I could put to the social worker and the doctor. Her idea was simple. As she has always said, use it or you will lose it. If the hours are there in my package, use them because you are not going to Level 4 if you still have hours leftover from Level 3. So this is the plan. Four daily two-hour shifts. Monday, Wednesday, and Friday to be used for personal care such as bathing. Thursday to be used as shopping day. On the three main days, the extra time leftover can be used for meal preparation and the cleaning of the unit. This plan was relayed to the social worker and the doctor which they were quite happy to accept as I won't be as independent as I used to be, and I'm getting the help that they think I need.

All that was left to see was a physiotherapist. I told her about my IBM and that if a muscle is dead, it cannot be revived; it does not matter what you do to it. As usual, she had never heard of IBM, had never come across a case in over 12 years. She said to me, "I can't help you. I would not know what to prescribe I will have to go and check up on this illness to see what I am dealing with." At least she was honest. You would think that a public hospital the size of Rosebud would have access to more experienced physiotherapists. I know the disease is rare but surely, there has to be some paraphernalia on the subject. You would think that the disease would be brought up in their training. Over the period of time since I have been diagnosed, a lot more people know about IBM. To be honest, I am getting sick and tired of telling doctors and nurses about it. Many of it I believe go in one ear and out the other. They only use it as a conversation piece at the time they are talking to you. Hopefully, word gets around and something can be done about it in the future.

Guess what, I'm going home. The doctor has just paid a visit and she said that they have everything under control with the nausea, and that the pain management for the ribs is also under control. She was also advised of my homecoming plan and agreed with everyone else that this will work, and I'm not going home to nothing. So at 4:00 o'clock in the afternoon, I was wheelchaired out of the place after being there for six days—an ordeal I would not wish on my worst enemy. I would give the nurses 10 out of 10. I would give the hospital 10 out of 10. I will give the doctors 9 out of 10. The food I have not rated; let's give it four out of 10. I know you go to the hospital when you are feeling shit, and it takes a few days of treatment to get over it all which we did and are very grateful. I cannot wait to get home to see my dog and cat.

Shane picked me up and it was great to be home and walk through that front door. Bo, at first, did not realise who I was until I went into the bedroom; he jumped onto the bed and the penny dropped he then knew who it was. He was so excited and not being a licker, he excelled himself; he could not stop kissing me. Oscar, the cat, also realised I was home. He jumped up as well and I had two of them to contend with how fantastic it was to get such a great greeting from two great animals. I love them dearly. Guess what we are having for dinner… KFC. I hope the stomach can contend with such a delicacy.

Now that I'm home, I will have to be content with the sleeping pills I have and not the hospital ones. Not that they worked anyway. I still had problems getting to sleep while in the hospital. The normal pills that I use are out of stock and have to order them through Amazon. I have some which I purchased from the chemist. I don't find them much good but I suppose they are better than nothing. I will give them a go tonight and see how they work.

CHAPTER 19

I went into Jeanette's front room and saw some of the junk laying around—one large piece being the lift and transfer chair. I thought I might try and resell it on eBay. Then I discovered the product can be returned for any legitimate reason. I felt that our reason was good enough in that she went into a nursing home before we could utilise the unit. Providing the unit had not been used and can fit nicely back into the box, eBay provided me with post details. Unbeknown to us, the cut-off point for Australia post is 23 kilos. This bloody thing weighed in at 24 kilos thus, we had to make private arrangements for the parcel to be picked up. Some people can be a pain in the bum to do business with. I emailed the people we purchased the product from, stating the reason why we wanted to return the goods and asked him if he could send us his return address as the eBay transaction did not have all the relevant details for the courier we chose. We're only two days away from Christmas, and he did not want the product delivered at that time. I then suggested between Christmas and the

New Year. "Would that be suitable?" He said he preferred the New Year. I had to remind him that eBay was the one that wanted the transaction completed before the 4th of January. The guy reluctantly gave me the details I required. I've got the vibes he was shitty about having to take the product back. The charge for the parcel organised online was $55.

So, we got onto the mob couriers. Please, they said they would pick it up the day before Christmas. That came and went and we still had the parcel on Christmas Day. It took them till the 28th to pick it up. Then a minor stuff up at the other end which turned out to be Sydney, and the parcel was finally delivered on the 4th. Hooray, thank God that was over and unbeknownst to me, the seller was able to take a 20% return fee which he took off the bill. It doesn't rain, but it pours. I look at it this way: getting $890 back is better than losing $1,100 so I will put this down to experience and be very careful when purchasing something like this again. I will make sure I will need it 100% before I purchase.

Later on, eBay asked me if I would fill in a survey relating to my experience with the latest transaction and how happy would I be to recommend eBay for anybody who wishes to purchase goods online. I must admit this came as a bit of a surprise, so all they did was provide a post sticker for the parcel which could not be used as the weight was too much. There was no way known that I could reverse that postage sticker; there is nowhere on the site to be able to do this, so that was just left hanging in the background. Also, eBay did not inform me, and I did not look either to see if it was there or not of the 20% seller's return fee. So, I gave them negative feedback just to let them know I was not a happy chappie.

When we have a look at what was purchased for Jeanette and what is left over, we have not done too bad. The main article left over is the hospital bed which we have decided to keep as we got rid of the queen-sized bed which was in the room when the hospital bed was ordered. I think it will come in handy if anybody wants to stay overnight.

When we knew that Jeanette was going into permanent care, Renee, our case manager, worked very quickly to try and use up some of the funds which were in the account, so she ordered a fold-up wheelchair which values at $899 and a whizbang Jay clinical cushion. These are ideal for anyone who sits down a lot such as in a wheelchair. This will eliminate any sores from developing; that also cost around about the $900 mark. I may as well get something out of the wreck. At least, she can use these articles in the nursing home.

My Aged Care did not muck around. A letter was sent out informing us of the cancellation of the package she was on and that all funding has stopped and that any monies left in the account will be returned to My Aged Care.

I had a very interesting time with the electric wheelchair which I had purchased. I found it was losing power. I had it on charge every night, looked on YouTube to see if I was doing it right which I was, so the only thing to do is ring up Ray from our local mobility shop. We organised for him to pick it up and have a look at it. He wanted to meet me at 7:30 a.m. "Hey mate, I am an old bugger. It's hard for me to arise at that time." I told him I would leave the garage door open for him, so when it was time to let Oscar out, I opened the garage door. He had made very little noise for when I had finally arisen at around 8:30, the chair was gone. I just have to wait for him to get back to me now. It took him about a week to look it over and give us the results. His prognosis was, seeing the chair had been laying around for a while without any use, the batteries had deteriorated to a stage where it could no longer hold a charge. The chair overall was in excellent condition and once the new batteries are fitted, you should get many years use out of it. The batteries are not a standard line which he keeps in stock. They come in at a cost of $780, and he would have to order them in for me, so we told him to go ahead and ring us when the product is fixed. He also said that this is the Rolls Royce of wheelchairs and that this particular model runs up to around about $12,500 to $13,500. The cushion alone is worth $1,000. Certainly got the buy of the century with that deal. The chair is about three years old. Ray said, "He is never around when deals like that are about, so I miss out again!"

Unfortunately, all this was happening while I was in the hospital. Shane kept me updated with what was going on; he did all the negotiating with Ray. The batteries were put in and they were put immediately on charge. This went on for nearly a week where it was not even touched so it would have been fully charged by the time I was ready to use it. Took the chair outside, ready to give it a good going over. Two of my neighbours were waiting for a demonstration so off I went. It reached a certain speed (slow) and then it would not go any faster. It was if the batteries were not holding the charge.

I summoned Ray. "What have you done to me? The batteries must not be any good." His main question was, "What settings have you got the chair on?" I told him how I set the chair up prior to driving off, so this is what I do: I put the chair seat in a lift position which will lift me up about four inches higher than normal. I then put the chair in the tilt position and tilt it a couple of inches which also makes me more comfortable. I then put the chair into drive mode and off I go. He was able to pinpoint the problem immediately. He said, "These chairs have an automatic cut-out system so that when you put the chair into the lift position, it automatically cuts the speed down. It is a safety precaution because if you drive the chair and it is too high, they do have a tendency to tip over on unlevel ground so the speed is automatically cut for you, avoiding any mishaps which could occur." So what I've learned about all this is that you can tilt the chair into any position and the speed is not affected but as soon as you heighten the chair, the speed is cut. I invited the neighbours over to have a look at my speed test; they were amazed that a wheelchair could go at such a speed. I did not have it on full speed as I did not want to cause myself any harm—very impressive all the same. I was able to put the proposition to Home care that seeing this was a repair to a product which they did not pay for because it was through eBay and that is a no, they should be able to come to the party and pay for the repairs. Renee put it to her boss and they agreed with me, so the amount of $790 was paid for from our package quite handy!

I will have to be very careful how I now utilise my package. The level has not changed; I am still on Level 3, but I have no longer got Jeanette and her package as a backup and vice versa. She was able to use mine and I was able to use hers. It is all different. Now, there is only one to work on. On the level that I am on, I should be able to continue at least eight and a half hours per week with the female carers, which would leave a couple of areas vacant, such as gardening once every eight to 10 weeks, a podiatrist once every 10 weeks. I would have to keep my finger on the pulse with Renee to make sure we do not go over our limit, and it's such a bloody terrific thing to have.

As mentioned earlier, the girls have now got three two-hour shifts and one two-and-a-half-hour shift, the latter being for shopping. We increased that by half an hour. Those two hours do not seem to be enough to plan everything and then do the shopping. I told my girls a little in-house joke that I had made up. Here it is: once the word had gotten out that Wayne would have to be physically bathed at least three times a week, you should've seen what happened. The phones melted; they just would not stop ringing with people wanting the job. I went to the front door after a knock; there's a queue of women lined up right down the driveway to the street, hoping that they would be the ones chosen for this delicate and once-in-a-million job. Look what's happening to you guys. The gig is handed to you on a platter; you don't know how lucky you are. I got a few laughs around here. Thought it was a pretty good joke. Denise said to me, "At least, you have still got your sense of humour."

It has taken awhile for everything to settle down since coming out of hospital. I'm very fortunate to have neighbours who's showing interest in what is going on with me. A couple of them are making me meals, knocking on the door regularly to see if I am okay. I just thought I would mention this: the novelty has worn off. No longer do the neighbours come and offer me food gifts; that lasted a whole two weeks.

The regular carers have settled down to the new roster. I'm settled in the mind a lot better than I was, and my outlook is a little different to what it was prior to going into hospital.

We've had a couple of problems with Jeanette at the nursing home where she is not getting the care that she should get. After several complaints, the hierarchy have made a few adjustments and things are starting to look up. She seems to have settled in quite well, and I can see her anytime I want. Lately, we have been taking Bo in with us to see his mum. All good. I don't know if he's happy to see his mum. She seems happy to see him. Bo definitely enjoys the outing.

CHAPTER 20

It has been a full-on couple of months. All these distractions have caused me to move away from my encounters with IBM. It has been very important to me to share as much as I possibly can with you which includes my daily life. I must share these things with you so that we can work out how I cope and what impact it has on my IBM. No matter what happens, I still have IBM, and I still have to deal with what it dishes up to me on a daily basis. My last daily report was on the 17th of November 2022. It is now February 2023. The only difference on the functional rating scale is my bathing. I was on number 2, and now I've gone down to number 1 which requires occasional assistance from a caregiver. I did mention prior that I was having trouble holding a towel and drying myself. This is virtually gone to a caregiver doing most of the drying.

I'm so glad that the IBM is moving at a very slow rate and progression is very slow. Unfortunately, I will have to repeat some of the things that I have mentioned in the past, keep myself posted on the progression of the IBM. With my case manager, Renee, and the caregivers, as well as some of the things we have purchased, I think I'm ready for the future. We have the hospital bed, the electric wheelchair, the foldup wheelchair already just in case the legs go on me. One of my biggest fears is waking up one day and being unable to walk. We will face that hurdle if and when we come to it. I do feel that my legs—even though I have the odd fall—are not getting any worse. They are skinny and have no meat on them. Fortunately, they are still holding me up. I just have to keep up the concentration when I walk. Actually, in everything I do, I must concentrate.

The upper arm and shoulders are still giving me grief. We do have the pain under control with a patch. I said I'm handling it okay. My forearm does not give me any grief at all; they just lack the strength required to lift things. My hands and fingers are my major problem. Where I used to be able to bend my fingers manually, I now find that a difficult task. I try and do it as often as I can as I feel this can help loosen the fingers. I'm finding it harder and harder to hold things in my hands. I'm forever dropping items that I hold. I find it very difficult to bend over as my balance is so insecure and when I bend, I wobble. I'm forever using my pickup gadget, hopefully alleviating the bending down. I find it nearly impossible to pick up something off the ground that I have dropped. I now find I'm asking for help more often.

While working at the kitchen bench, the challenge is

not to drop anything while I'm preparing salad for dinner. As mentioned earlier, I'm now getting used to frozen precooked meals. I like having a salad on the side. Cutting food up is now a major hurdle. I find it very difficult to hold the knife straight and even having the strength to cut is a challenge. I have been told that I can now buy pre-cut salads which they sell at the supermarket. I think this is certainly going to be an option.

Another example of struggling to do a small task: yesterday, the caregiver hung the washing on the line to dry. When dry, I thought I would take them off the line and bring them in. Squeezing the peg was hard, but I was able to do it. Taking a shirt from the line and hanging it over my arm was okay, until I come to the third and fourth item. That is when the weight of the clothes became too much for my arm to hold; the only option was to take them inside and start again. Probably the easier way would have been to have a trolley to put the clothes in and take inside. Maybe next time. I continued the job until it was all done of course.

Tried making a bed the other day. I did not have the strength to lift the doona into position. That job has now been left to the caregiver. I'm still able to dress myself. Still have trouble with shoes. Needs a shoe horn and special shoelaces to make it work. I also have little difficulty putting socks on, lifting my arms to put a shirt on, test the shoulders and upper arms. Everything else, I'm able to do okay.

I now have caregivers helping me in the shower. I do what they call the Navy shower. Hop in the shower, water yourself down, turn the water off, have the girls soap myself down, rinse off—an easy way to save water then dry.

I am now doing everything a lot slower. I do not race into doing anything as the IBM has made sure that I do everything slower. What do they say? Slow and steady wins the race. Let's hope so. One area I did not mention is that I have now a full grey beard. Why? I find it very difficult to hold the razor so I thought it's easier to grow a beard. Why not?!

My physical shape has changed a little. I now weigh around 77 kilos. I am as skinny as a rake, and my frame makes me look like a prisoner of war. Remember the Holocaust when the people were rescued? They were nothing but skin and bones. That's me—nothing but skin and bones. Let's hope I can survive it..

Today is the 15th of February 2023. I hope you have enjoyed what I've written and I have enjoyed writing. It is very hard to pass on to people what happens to your body when you get whatever. I have noticed that since writing this book, there were a number of people who have spoken to me and told me of their ailments. I did mention it earlier that once you hit 70, the problem starts. They may be minor or they maybe major. We'll deal with these problems our own way. I hope you now know a little bit about IBM.

All we have to contend with now is the rotten IBM, how bad it is. Now from the time when I first started, how much worse will it get by the time it's finished. God only knows. I feel I'm relatively lucky that the disease is a slow progression. I feel at the moment the IBM is having small snooze and not progressing anywhere at this stage. If there are any changes in the body in the last three months, it has to be the hands. They are slightly stiffer. That's the only difference I feel at the moment, so I'm only hoping that it stays asleep and even dies, and then it does not raise its ugly head again. We all know unfortunately it will.

All I know is that I'm ready for whatever the good Lord wants to throw at me. BRING IT ON.

A question was asked............

HOW DO YOU COPE WITH THIS?

The answer............

THAT IS HOW I COPED WITH THIS!

www.ingramcontent.com/pod-product-compliance
Lightning Source LLC
LaVergne TN
LVHW091544060526
838200LV00036B/699